A PSYCHIC TO THE RESCUE

Twenty-six women had been brutalized. Police teams were frustrated in their efforts to catch the criminal, who invariably wore a blue ski mask.

Police officer Gary Robinson had been sent to ask for Sylvia Brown's help.

"I can see him!" she exclaimed. "He's husky, dark-haired . . . his last name begins with an *S*. It's going to happen next in Redwood City. He wants to rape someone there, but instead you'll catch him."

Two weeks later, police arrested a man named Sanchez breaking into a Redwood City home where a woman lived alone. He was wearing a ski mask. Now he is serving a life term in prison, thanks to Sylvia Brown.

"ENJOYABLE . . . EMINENTLY READABLE."
—Booklist

Sylvia Brown is a psychic and the president of the Nirvana Foundation for Psychic Research. She is a regular guest on San Francisco's "People Are Talking" and "Good Morning, LA." Sylvia Brown's Church of Novus Spiritus is located in Campbell, CA, (800) 966-4600. **Antoinette May** is an author and journalist. Her books include *Witness to War*, *Haunted Houses* and *Wandering Ghosts of California*.

Adventures of a Psychic

(formerly titled *My Guide, Myself*)

by
Sylvia Brown
and Antoinette May

A SIGNET BOOK

SIGNET
Published by the Penguin Group
Penguin Books USA Inc., 375 Hudson Street,
New York, New York 10014, U.S.A.
Penguin Books Ltd, 27 Wrights Lane,
London W8 5TZ, England
Penguin Books Australia Ltd, Ringwood,
Victoria, Australia
Penguin Books Canada Ltd, 2801 John Street,
Markham, Ontario, Canada L3R 1B4
Penguin Books (N.Z.) Ltd, 182–190 Wairau Road,
Auckland 10, New Zealand

Penguin Books Ltd, Registered Offices:
Harmondsworth, Middlesex, England

Published by Signet, an imprint of New American Library, a division of
Penguin Books USA Inc. Previously published under the title *My Guide, Myself*
by NAL BOOKS, an imprint of New American Library, a division of
Penguin Books USA Inc.

First Signet Printing, August, 1991
10 9 8 7 6 5 4 3 2 1

 REGISTERED TRADEMARK—MARCA REGISTRADA

Printed in the United States of America

This book owes its existence
most directly to a special friend
and mentor, John Wilson,
whose editorial skill and creative
instincts once again proved invaluable.
—ANTOINETTE MAY

_____

This book is dedicated to
my grandmother,
Ada Coil
who provided the
wind which
filled the sail.

A special thanks to my sons
Paul and Chris
for their love and support
and to a special friend,
Larry Beck.
—SYLVIA BROWN

Contents

Foreword by Sylvia Brown	1
Introduction by Antoinette May	5
1. People are Talking	9
2. Francine's Friend	18
3. A Psychic in Love	35
4. Growing Pains	57
5. Following the Blueprint	72
6. Nirvana	94
7. The Other Side	105
8. The Reading Room	128
9. Haunting Expressions	139
Ghost-Hunting Protocol	163
10. Mumbi-One	165
Life Themes	191
11. Medicine and the Medium	203
The Laboratory Technique	214
12. The Psychic Detective	216
The Temple of Quiet	225
13. Novus Spiritus	227
The Tenets of Novus Spiritus	237

Foreword

I HAD many reasons for wanting this book written, but two of my primary goals deserve special mention. First of all I wanted to give people an understanding of what a psychic is truly all about. Being psychic is a family pattern which includes my grandmother Ada Coil, an uncle, and my youngest son Christopher Dufresene. The genetic aspect is important, but it is not the truest measure of what being psychic really entails. The real issues revolve around our trials and tribulations, our heartaches and struggles, and the tempering of our souls to make us a vehicle for God.

Secondly, this is a story about a woman. One who is perhaps (is this a crime?) too giving, too naive, too understanding, and too selfless. Yet this woman is very intelligent, a type of savant almost, as far as people's lives, truth, and spirituality are concerned. I also want to show that a religious or spiritual person is also very human, not saintly, and will experience the same hurts, deceptions, fears, and phobias as everyone else.

Psychics are really just human beings with a gift, which does not serve us personally very well. I have found, as I get older, the gift is not for my benefit in any way, shape, or form. It is something to be given away. If psychics could benefit from their gift, they would simply win the big lotto and never do what they are supposed to do—help others.

My life reads like a struggle for survival, as do most lives. There are loves that went unrequited, challenges met, deceptions at the hands of friends, and people who hurt me. I think that my story is every man's story, it is every woman's story. I hope that it is a story of bravery, because I have certainly had to be brave, strong, and sometimes, in the very bottom of my heart, very frightened, alone, and childlike.

Mine is a story of faith, a woman's faith in her God, and her Goddess. I came here to herald the first wave of the Gnostic Way, which is the most ancient quest of man searching for truth and his own spirituality. Where Nirvana and Novus Spiritus go from here is only known to God. As for me, I will always be helping people, always guiding as God sees fit. If I must do my work from the back of a goat cart, I will. My contract with God must be fulfilled.

You will see that this book is written with humor. You will see the friendship between Antoinette and me that spans fifteen years. You will see the love and respect we have for each other, you will see that there are many things yet to come as surprises, not only for you, but even for me. Bear with me in this odyssey, bear with me in this journey. Understand and try to see beyond just the written word to the heart of the woman, the heart of the person, who possibly is too naive, too understanding, and too giving, but certainly has a lot of guts.

For all of you who toil in little dark corners, remember me sometimes, this girl from Missouri. I did not necessarily "make good," but I certainly gave it my all. I think that God simply wants us to give it our all, give it our best shot. So this is a book of friendship, this is a book about loyalty, pain, heartache, and challenges. It is everyone's story. Would I have changed any of it? I had to think hard on that, but I think not. Someone told me that I am a "karmic catharsis" for everyone, which seems to fit well.

I know that we all learn by experiencing and watching how a life unfolds; I hope you enjoy mine, and can learn faster than I did.

God love you, I do . . .

—SYLVIA BROWN

Introduction

THE first time I met Sylvia Brown—and her spirit guide, Francine—was at a séance in my living room. A small psychic research group gathered there on a weekly basis in the 1970s, an outgrowth of a parapsychology class that I was teaching at a nearby community college.

All of us—psychologists, lawyers, real estate appraisers, writers, editors, educators and salespersons—were fascinated by the possibilities of this "new" science. All of us were eager to learn more about the other world of the paranormal; and, in so doing, learn more about ourselves.

We experimented wtih a variety of ESP tests and meditative techniques; we were regressed to past lives, had our auras photographed by Kirlian cameras, observed spoon benders, healers, and plant communicators. Some of what we saw and did was impressive, some strained credulity.

In the fall of 1975, shortly after publication of an article I'd written for *Psychic Magazine*, I received a telephone call. "The mediums that you wrote about were interesting," said the woman, a stranger, "but I know someone far more gifted. When you meet her—when you see what she can do—you'll want to write about *her*."

Perhaps my caller, too, was a little psychic.

Our group was excited about the prospects of a séance. Few had attended one. None of us had heard of Sylvia and had no idea of what to expect. Envisioning a Madame

Lazonga type with cape and turban, we were unprepared for the lively, down-to-earth woman who appeared with her handsome husband, Dal.

Dal explained that Sylvia would be leaving her body while Francine, her spirit guide, entered it. "It's Francine, not Sylvia, who will be answering your questions."

"I've spent so much time out of my body waiting for Francine to get through talking that I began to hope that it might impede the aging process," Sylvia admitted.

"Has it?" we all wanted to know.

"Not a damn bit."

Sylvia lay down on the couch, a pillow under her head. "It's necessary to be very quiet as she goes under, but afterwards you can make as much noise as you like," Dal explained to us.

We sat silently, expectantly waiting for something to happen. At first nothing did. I studied the woman on the couch. She was lying absolutely still. As I watched it seemed that slowly, almost imperceptibly, Sylvia's features began to change. Her face seemed broader, flatter, the large dark eyes less prominent; the eyelids now seemed slightly hooded.

"Francine's here with us now, she's inside Sylvia," Dal announced. "You can ask her anything you like."

When the others hesitated, I plunged in. Having just completed a book, I was curious about what my next project would be.

"It will be another book," Francine told me in the precise, almost stilted manner which I learned was characteristic of her. "You will be working on it very soon. You are going to take the back of a book—something that you have already written and rearrange it with something new. What was the back will be the front. Something unused before will be part of a new book." (And that's exactly what happened.)

Suddenly there were many questions. Everyone had

something to ask about health, about money, about career choices, about relationships—particularly about relationships.

"Will I *ever* get along with my mother?" a middle-aged woman asked.

"No, your mother will always be difficult," Francine replied. "She is a very critical woman. She gives you many mixed messages. Nothing you do satisfies her."

"Why that's *my* mother you're talking about!" another woman exclaimed.

"No, it's mine," someone else said.

"Sounds more like mine," yet another voice insisted.

Soon everyone was laughing at the recognition of this common problem shared by so many—everyone, that is, but the woman on the couch, who remained silent, unperturbed. Francine didn't laugh; nor, of course, did Sylvia.

When the laughter finally stopped, the spirit guide continued. "It is best for you to keep in mind that tolerance for your mother's impossible demands will enable you to move toward your own perfection."

Later, when the séance was over and Sylvia had reappeared, I told her what had happened. "I miss everything," she lamented. "It must have been funny, but actually that description—it sounds like *my* mother."

That evening was the beginning of an enduring friendship. Sylvia's unique combination of humor, strength, courage, and insight has enriched my life in many ways—as has Francine's wisdom. I've spent a number of long nights with Sylvia in haunted houses, watching as she quite literally called forth the dead; I've observed her work with doctors and with the police. At the same time, the nature of my own work has brought me in contact with a number of gifted psychics.

There is no one that I trust and respect more than Sylvia Brown. Her story of triumph over adversity is truly inspiring. The wisdom that she has received from Francine brings meaning and order into the seeming random chaos of life. Francine's path is one of both compassion and ultimate transcendence. Anyone can follow that path; everyone can benefit from it.

—ANTOINETTE MAY
Palo Alto, California

CHAPTER ONE

People Are Talking

THE capacity audience is restless, eager. This isn't just any TV show. These people seek more than entertainment. They want answers.

The excitement is palpable as the lights brighten, the theme music goes on. The studio audience stamps and cheers without prompting as the ebullient host, Ross McGowan, announces, "Today we have with us the internationally known psychic, our own Sylvia Brown."

The rotating stage moves on cue, stopping with a sudden jerk to reveal a Junoesque woman with warm brown eyes that seem to dominate her entire face. There's a burst of spontaneous applause. In the trade, Sylvia Brown is known as "good TV" because the ratings invariably zoom when she appears.

Ann Fraser, the attractive blonde cohost, steps forward. Scanning the excited audience, she asks, "Is there anyone here who doesn't believe in psychics?"

A tall, dark man raises his hand defiantly. "There's some kind of dairy farm that you'll be going into," Sylvia tells him. "You have two sons, but are raising two other boys as well." Her smile broadens at the familiar look of astonishment. Then she adds, "You should check the transmission on your car and see a doctor about that left knee."

The man stares at her, surprise and confusion apparent in his face.

"Does any of this hit home?" Ann Fraser asks.

"I wish you'd go to someone else. This is kind of spooky," he answers.

"What do you mean 'spooky'?" Ann persists.

The man talks so softly that he has to be urged to speak up. "I just learned last night that I'd inherited a dairy farm. I took my car into the garage this morning and was told that the transmission's shot. My knee has been hurting a lot these days, an old football injury acting up. I have two sons and those other two boys—well, I'd rather not talk about them."

And so it goes for voyeurs at home as well as for the studio audience. People wave wildly for the mike, eager to discuss their tangled love lives, their rare diseases, their finances, their neurotic families. Sylvia's mobile face plays at martyrdom, her eyes rolling comically. Her presence is large and maternal, her style fast and frequently profane. Even skeptics are drawn to her warmth and compassion.

An older, gray-haired woman stands, her arms almost hugging her chest. "Some of what you say seems kind of general to me," she accuses. "When you tell someone they're going to move—couldn't that apply to anyone in California?"

"Possibly," Sylvia concedes. "But suppose I say to you, 'you moved last month into a white stucco house with blue trim.' Is that general? Of course not. General is, 'you're moving from darkness into the light.'"

The woman's jaw drops. "You—you're right," she stammers. "I did move, that's my house."

"It was a good move," Sylvia assures her. "You're going to be happy there."

"One thing you can say," the woman concedes, "it's certainly good show biz."

"Yeah," Sylvia agrees. "There is a little entertainment in what I do, but most of it is 'heal fast and make well.' I'm a fast-foods psychic. Fast food means you come in, you get what you need to get healed, and then you walk out the door. It's a kind of battlefield situation. Life is a kind of battlefield."

The audience oohs and aahs as the TV show continues, but this is the easy stuff. The information Sylvia divulges can be verified instantly. The real work comes when the sensitive goes into the future precognitively and talks about things that are beyond present awareness. The subjects shake their heads doubtfully. "Me, another baby! I'll be forty-five in December. No way!" Or, "Move to Minnesota? You've got to be kidding. It wouldn't matter how good the job was." The verification will come later, sometimes much later. Sylvia will receive a call and be told, "Remember me, I was the one you said . . . Well, I just wanted to tell you . . ."

The local CBS-TV show is aptly named *People Are Talking*. People *are* talking about Sylvia Brown. But more precisely, they come to talk about themselves—their hopes, their fears, sometimes even their secrets. It's not new. The questions asked of this modern seer are identical to those placed before the Delphic oracles thousands of years ago. Only the delivery system has changed.

A pretty red-haired woman stands up, waving eagerly at Sylvia. "I'd like to ask something for my girlfriend and myself," she says. "My friend's thirty and wants to get married. I'm a little younger; right now I'd be happy with a meaningful relationship. Do you see anyone coming into either of our lives?"

"Yes," Sylvia nods emphatically, "but you'll marry first."

"Ooh! Me first! Is it the guy I met on the cruise—blonde, a little taller than me?"

"No, hon, someone else. A big, tall guy, handsome."

"Mmm, sounds good." The young woman sits down, smiling happily.

"He sounds good to me, too," Sylvia says as her eyes brighten mischievously to the color of warm sherry.

The girl stands up again. "My friend—"

"Yes, hon, she'll marry too, but not for five years."

An older woman raises her hand timidly and then, encouraged by Sylvia, begins slowly, tentatively. "I lost a baby three years ago," she declares. "It was a crib death. Why did it happen?"

"The timing wasn't right for either of you. Who are we to question that? The entity came through briefly to help you with your spiritual perfection—someone who was close to you before. The two of you made an agreement to be together for just a little while."

"But I want another child. Will I ever—?"

"What day is it?"

"I think I could be . . . maybe . . ."

"That's what I'm saying. You're already there."

The woman virtually shrieks with happy excitement. The whole audience is clapping wildly. When the noise subsides, Sylvia informs her, "It'll be another boy."

Ann Fraser looks at Sylvia in surprise. "She didn't say the child was a boy."

Sylvia laughs. "She didn't have to—remember me, I'm Sylvia Brown."

Sylvia uses the same telepathic shorthand in the next question. "I was in a bad accident a year ago—" a short, stocky man begins. A medical problem is anticipated by everyone, but Sylvia knows better. Before he can frame his query, she has interrupted him. "Yes, you'll come out well on that," she predicts. When the man pauses in surprise, Sylvia encourages him. "Your lawsuit. You'll do very well. Don't change lawyers. The one you've got— the tall, bald guy—he's very good. Keep him."

Sylvia's manner is frequently flip, funny, often suggestive of a stand-up comic, but underlying it all is a warmth and compassion that draws skeptic and believer alike. Always Sylvia speaks in specifics and shoots from the hip.

Now looking about the studio, she spots a woman sitting on the aisle near the back. "You're concerned, aren't you? About something that may even approach blackmail," she suggests. "Don't pay it. None of what's happened is as it appears to you now. He's playing on your fears. Call him on it and he'll drop the whole business." The woman's face brightens. Her relief is obvious. "Thank you," she murmurs.

These are the happy, easy answers. The more traumatic ones are harder to deal with, especially on television. Often the messages Sylvia delivers are carefully couched. "I see two pregnancies this year," she tells a young woman who hopes to conceive a child. "Don't feel bad about the first. The second will be a girl—born early next spring." The word miscarriage isn't used.

But other times Sylvia is more direct. "That new red sports car you're so crazy about—get rid of it *right away*," she warns a glitzy brunette.

Eventually, there are questions about Sylvia herself. "It sounds like you believe in reincarnation," a man ventures.

"I don't believe," she answers. "I know. God's an equal-opportunity employer. Do you think he'd give us just one chance?"

"How long have you felt that way?"

"Always, I guess. When I was three, I'd insist that my father taste my food first. They tell me I'd sit very patiently watching him chew, waiting. When nothing happened, I'd dive in—I've always had quite an appetite. It must have been hard for me to wait; but I did. Apparently I had a strong memory of being poisoned in a past life and wasn't about to make that mistake again. Maybe I sensed even then that I had lots to acomplish this time around."

Most children are born with past-life recall, Sylvia believes, but they can't pass on the information available to them for lack of vocabulary. Impatient or skeptical parents compound the problem, so unfortunately much valuable information is lost forever because, as we grow older, we tend to forget.

"What's it like to be psychic?" a young man calls out from the back of the studio.

"What's it like *not* to be psychic?" she asks, shrugging. "I've always known things without being told. When I was only five or so my father took me to the drugstore and sat me down in front of some picture books while he went off somewhere. Suddenly I had a very clear picture of him in my mind, talking on the phone. I could see the person he was talking to as well—a pretty blonde woman whom I didn't know. Poor Daddy! When I got home, I told the whole family all about it. The silence was deafening—at least while I was present. The next day Daddy started out the door with his fishing rod. What a little fink I was! 'He isn't really going fishing,' I told my mother. 'He's going on a trip with his girlfriend.' That afternoon my grandmother, who also had the gift, gave me a long lecture on psychic etiquette."

This was only the beginning of a rapidly unfolding drama, as some of the fans in the audience already know. "What about your spirit guide?" someone asks. The questioner is a scholarly looking woman in a far corner. "What about Francine?"

Even the regulars lean forward expectantly. For them it's a familiar but still fascinating story. "I was eight when Francine first appeared to me," Sylvia explains. "I can't remember when I didn't hear messages that others couldn't, but they were always far off in the background, almost like a soft whisper that could be ignored. Francine was something else entirely. One night I was lying in bed playing with a flashlight when suddenly I saw this Indian woman.

" 'Don't be afraid, Sylvia, I come from God,' she said.

Don't be afraid! She was as close, as real, as—as—Ann Fraser," Sylvia insists, pointing to the woman sitting beside her. "And there she was standing right in the middle of my bedroom. I jumped up and ran out screaming. Fortunately—is there really such a thing as fortune or chance?—my psychic grandmother was staying with us. She was very ho-hum about it all. And that was reassuring to me. She explained that we all have spirit guides who are assigned to us as helpers. The only difference was that she and I could see ours."

Sylvia's guide is a South American Indian whose name in life was Iena. "That was a little too bizarre for an eight-year-old," Sylvia remembers. "I liked the name Francine, so that's what I rechristened my new friend. She didn't mind; in fact, she seemed to know exactly the sort of things that would appeal to me. I lost my fear of her completely when she taught me to play 'What are they saying downstairs?' You can imagine the stir that game created, but it was a nice stir. Francine, like Grandma, was and is the quintessence of psychic etiquette. In the beginning, she seemed very old to me—she was about thirty and there she remains."

It was difficult at first to accustom herself to Francine's thought patterns, Sylvia says. "She's so literal compared to us, I'm still sometimes surprised. For instance, if I were to ask her, 'Can you describe yourself?' Francine would just say, 'Yes,' and stop there. In reply to someone's question about a forthcoming holiday, she'd just say something like, 'I see you going to the high country to hook animals.' We'd interpret that as a fishing trip in the mountains."

Ross McGowan asks a question for the audience. "Don't you sometimes feel that what you tell people robs them of their free will?" he inquires.

Sylvia shakes her head. "Absolutely not. If I get it, you're supposed to know. I believe that what I receive comes from God, just as Francine told me long ago." She laughs good-naturedly. "I'd hate to think it was coming from me!"

Specifics are essential, she believes. "That's what mediumship is all about. I wouldn't be a professional if I told people all that Mickey Mouse stuff about going from darkness into the light. *Anybody* can say something like that, but what good does it do? You can't help someone without giving specific information. Francine comes through when I'm in the trance state and tells people about their soul work, what their mission in life is, their themes and patterns. I stay with the now, the gritty soap opera of life."

Sometimes with Francine's help and at other times without it, Sylvia is able to tune into the "blueprint" within each of her subjects. Though she prefers to do one-on-one predictions, she has acquired a national reputation for general-interest forecasts. "It's really no different," she tells the audience. "I just sit down and ask myself questions. What about the economy? What about the president's health? What about earthquakes? What about—"

"What about my report card?" a small boy cries out.

"Something's dragging and it's not P.E.," Sylvia warns him.

Though she has scant interest in sports, Sylvia is always in demand to predict winners. Her success rate here is amazing. "I don't think I was even aware of the Super Bowl until people began asking me about it," she admits. "Now I've picked the last five winners in a row. A few years back, I announced that the Oakland Raiders would be moving. Then they did. People were outraged. You should have seen the letters I got. You'd have thought I did it myself." She shrugs her shoulders in a familiar gesture of resignation.

"But how do you do it?" Ann Fraser asks.

"I don't know," Sylvia confides. "I really don't. I just open myself up and it comes. I don't analyze. Like once

I told a woman that she was going to start a worm farm. Yes, a worm farm! If I'd thought about that I wouldn't have said it, but I *didn't* think, I just opened my mouth and out it came—exactly what I was receiving. The woman wasn't surprised at all. 'Yeah,' she said, 'I always thought that would be an interesting way to make a living.' "

An older man rises to ask one last question. "What about you, Sylvia. What's in your future?"

Sylvia shakes her head, the honey-blonde hair gleaming under the TV lights. "I never know. The gift isn't meant for the medium herself. If I weren't doing the right thing it would all shut down. People ask me if I ever get bored answering the same old questions. The answer's no, I certainly don't. If it's important to the subject, it's important to me. People are funny, though. Once I told a man he'd be starting a new job on April fifth and he called indignantly to tell me I was all wrong—it had been April sixth."

"But don't you *ever* see anything for yourself?" the questioner persists.

"Very rarely," she answers firmly, "and I'm glad it's that way." For an instant, Sylvia's face clouds as her thoughts turn unbidden to a tragic love affair long ago. There *had* been a warning.

Ross signals. It's commercial time. A brief windup and the show is over. Sylvia is smiling again at the audience as the revolving stage moves her backward into the shadows.

CHAPTER TWO

Francine's Friend

IT was nearly midnight and Sylvia Brown was on her way to the séance. As her car hugged the narrow, winding road which snaked its way along the craggy seacoast, she smiled wryly.

Did fiction strive to emulate truth or was it actually the other way around? Tonight was the proverbial dark and stormy night. A few miles to the north, twelve people waited for her in a century-old farmhouse. She would be the thirteenth. There were some—certain San Francisco press members among them—who believed the house was haunted. How sensational—even terrifying—it all sounded! For Sylvia, it was neither. Fiction—truth? Truth—fiction?

The windshield wipers beat valiantly against the driving rain. Grateful for the presence of the man at the wheel beside her, Sylvia leaned back, eyes closed, thoughts wandering.

It had been an exhausting day, beginning with an early-morning distress call. A child was missing. Sylvia's psychic insights had scarcely enabled the San Jose Police Department to bring the mystery to a happy conclusion before another case developed—the unidentified body of a teen-age girl.

Reluctantly, Sylvia had focused on the tragedy. In her mind's eye she "saw" a pretty blonde lying half-clothed and bleeding on the shoulder of a busy freeway. "Anderson," Sylvia had told the police officer. "Her last name's Anderson. Her first name begins with C—Carol, maybe, no, Carey—Carolyn. I'm not sure. But she knew the killer; she'd gotten into his car. He was angry, jealous. That's all I'm getting," she'd apologized. It had been enough. The case was well on the way to solution.

Then there'd been the regularly scheduled readings. Eight clients that day in her Nirvana Foundation office. Some insights had been pleasant—the whereabouts of an heirloom ring pinpointed. Another had been humorous— the raging temperature of a canny but less than intellectual boy explained by a hot water faucet. Some after-school tutoring would take care of him. Sylvia sighed as she thought of another client, a woman whose illness was terminal. What could one offer her but honesty, compassion, and a faith in the continuity of the human spirit?

The ghost-chasing expedition that had brought Sylvia to this desolate strip of the northern California coast came into sharp perspective. There had been so much chatter about ghosts of late, so many macabre headlines, such a proliferation of films, both humorous and horrible. Surely no one could deny that the very mention of the word exerts a fascination.

Sylvia was well aware that this enterprise might amount to little more than a parlor game, yet there was always the chance that there was some substance to the strange set of circumstances that had resulted in her summons. She hoped the séance would be productive. Often they evoked startling revelations, but, she reminded herself, just as often they proved to be dull time-wasters. She smiled, recalling the numerous nights her tape recorders had picked up the very mortal snores of witnesses who'd grown weary waiting until nearly dawn for something to happen.

Whatever might occur that night, the facts of life and the anomaly of death were very clear to Sylvia. Long ago she'd discovered that people don't die at all. They only die to you. That was the sad part, the hard part, the lesson forced upon her when she was scarcely more than a toddler.

Today Sylvia Brown can truly say that her best and *closest* friend has long been "dead." It wasn't always so simple.

Does present-day truth lie hidden in the ancient traditions of the Old Ones? Perhaps. Sylvia Celeste Shoemaker was born October 19, 1936 in Kansas City, Missouri. Her arrival was like that of any other baby, except that she was born with a caul.

When wrapped about the head of a newborn infant, a caul—the inner fetal membrane—has for centuries signified the birth of a child with the "sight," that inner seeing, inner *knowing*, that distinguishes the psychic from all others.

Bill Shoemaker, Sylvia's father, who attended the birth, already had a psychic mother-in-law to contend with. Now here was another psychic in the family. When the caul was removed, yet another mystical portent was revealed. On the forehead of his baby daughter, centered just above her two great brown eyes, was a tiny drop of blood. It looked for all the world like the mysterious third eye— the all-seeing orb of the prophet.

Sylvia has come to believe that everyone is psychic, but most people remain unaware of their own extra sensory abilities. It's possible that the presence of a caul may be a reminder to those whose lives will require a greater use of their gift. For Sylvia, the ancient sign was prophetic. She seems never to have known what it was like *not* to be psychic.

The "signs" appeared very early. It would seem that she was being prepared for the extraordinary path ahead. Sylvia *knew* who was at the door—before the guest even knocked. Then when she was three, Bill's father died suddenly of a heart attack. Bill learned of the tragedy at work and came home to inform his wife, Celeste. Sylvia was standing in the doorway when he entered. "Grandpa's dead," she announced before her father had uttered a word.

A far happier pronouncement was Sylvia's prediction that a baby sister was joining them. "She'll come in three years—when I'm six," she announced. Sharon arrived one month short of her sister's sixth birthday. Sylvia hears these stories told and retold at family gatherings, but can only smile at the continuing sense of marvel. What did they expect of a child building psychic muscle?

A far more important event occurred when Sylvia was four. Early one morning, hearing her postman father depart for his early-morning mail route, Sylvia trotted into her parents' room and climbed into bed beside her mother. Suddenly, as the tiny child glanced randomly at the ceiling, it burst open before her eyes. High above her was a glorious sunrise, with streaks of cerise, gold, hot pink, and purple against the somber dawn. Soaring across this grand panorama was a flock of wild birds flying in a V-formation. A voice spoke with great clarity, *"Sylvia, you will never be free as the birds you see."*

"Did you hear that?" she asked her mother in astonishment. "What happened to the ceiling? Do you see those birds?"

Celeste Shoemaker had seen nothing. As the daughter of a medium, she'd grown up in a home where visions were commonplace. Although not psychic herself, paranormal phenomena were nothing new to her. Celeste's attitude toward Sylvia's growing "strangeness" was one of mild annoyance. She didn't welcome more eccentricity in her life and would do nothing to encourage it in her daughter.

The ceiling looked exactly as it always had, Celeste assured Sylvia, and she attempted to divert the child's attention with talk of breakfast.

But Sylvia never forgot the experience. In later years, recalling the free-flowing momentum of the birds, the full realization of the message was revealed to her. The word *freedom* has many meanings to as many people, but psychics are the first to agree that they themselves have very little freedom indeed.

Sylvia believes that people chosen to be psychic must share their gift—at whatever cost to their own comfort or peace of mind. For some, perhaps, lifelong dedication comes easy, but for her, it has not. The suffering has often been intense—particularly when the "gift" has come into open conflict with her own desires.

The unwanted knowing began when Sylvia was five. The family was assembled for a Sunday gathering. Sylvia was seated beside her father listening halfheartedly to the adult chatter. Glancing absently at Great-Grandmother Hattie, who was seated across from her, she was horrified to see the woman's face begin to slowly melt. Her features were running like wax, slowly oozing downward until there was no face—only a skull.

Screaming her terror, the child turned only to confront the face of her other great-grandmother, Sarah. It, too, appeared to be melting—not as rapidly, but melting nevertheless. Frantically, Sylvia pulled at her father's arm, begging him to take her home. Outside, she attempted to explain to him the frightful thing she'd witnessed. "I saw their faces running," the little girl sobbed. He would not, could not, understand her.

Within ten days Hattie Braun was dead. Four days later, Sarah Shoemaker's death followed. Sylvia began to see other melting faces, and each vision was invariably followed by death. Her fear and confusion led to feelings of guilt. Was she in some way responsible? Sylvia was miserable. Again and again she tried to explain these happenings to parents too involved in their own affairs to recognize the enormity of what the child was experiencing.

Bill Shoemaker was ambitious, determined to get ahead in the world. He was also a charmer who found little difficulty balancing a philandering nature with conventional family responsibilities. Celeste was challenged by a Don Juan husband seven years her junior, but she had determined to wait it out. "One day Bill will grow up," she often sighed. In the meantime, her method of dealing with problems was to pretend they didn't exist.

Sylvia would vividly recall her mother's response to anything remotely threatening. Celeste simply excused herself and slipped off to have a long soak in the bathtub. It was a family signal that she'd insulated herself from reality and was not to be disturbed. During those traumatic days of melting faces, Celeste took many baths while Bill indulged himself with a passing parade of pretty ladies.

Then one day Sylvia's maternal grandmother, Ada Coil, came to call. Seating herself beside the frightened child, who was daily growing more and more withdrawn, she pulled the now-sobbing girl into her lap and comforted her. When the tears had subsided, Ada began to question her granddaughter gently and with great care.

Once again, Sylvia attempted to describe what she'd seen—the running, oozing faces slipping slowly downward until nothing remained but a skull. "Am I killing them, Grandma?" the child asked, her voice little more than a whisper.

"No, dear, it's their time to go. You have nothing to do with it," the older woman assured her.

"Then it *is* real?"

"Very real."

"Do you see the melting faces, too?" Sylvia asked, leaning forward conspiratorially.

"Not the faces, but other things. I see much that others don't—just as you do. It's because we're psychic."

Five-year-old Sylvia didn't want to be psychic. It wasn't

fun at all! Patiently, Ada explained that the gift of sight was theirs—want it or not. It was a kind of trust to be used for the benefit of others.

"But I don't *want* to see melting faces, I'm afraid of skulls," Sylvia said, beginning to cry again.

"Then ask God not to show them to you," Ada advised. "What you can't handle, pray to be relieved of."

The young Sylvia did a lot of praying. The hideous visions have never returned.

Tall, stately, dominant, Ada Coil was a true mentor, providing both practical solace for this world and a magic thread to guide Sylvia through the dark labyrinth of the other. A German from the noble Rhine family of von Banica, she had taken the name Coil from her Irish husband. She was a devout Lutheran, but always a pragmatist.

The Shoemaker family was divided. Bill was a Jew, Celeste an Episcopalian. Harmony was not the most notable household characteristic. Something had to be done about their daughter. Sylvia clearly needed stability and guidance. Ultimately, the idea of a convent emerged as the perfect solution. So at Grandma's urging, the Shoemakers became a Catholic family, with Ada taking instruction along with Bill, Celeste, and Sylvia. Ada had envisioned the entire family marching down the aisle to be baptized together and that's exactly what happened.

Sylvia adapted quickly to Catholic teaching. She was particularly impressed by the nuns and strove to emulate them. Soon there was a makeshift altar in her bedroom and for days at a time the child insisted on wearing a long black dress with a white tea towel pinned to it. No one was surprised when she announced that she wanted to be a nun.

Like Grandma Ada, the nuns appeared to Sylvia as islands of strength and clarity in a world that was becoming more and more complex. Bright, eager both to learn and to please, Sylvia found that school was easy although other things were not. Her increasing psychic abilities were a burden from which she could never free herself, separating her from friends and parents alike. More than anything, the child wanted to be "normal."

She had begun to see "inside" her head, frequently experiencing an eerie montage of spirits and mortals, two distinct vibrations going on simultaneously. Often she would ask people—anyone who happened to be near— "Did you see that?" The answer was always No.

What a relief it was to her when Grandma Ada provided unexpected validation. It was after dinner one Sunday evening. Family members gathered in the Shoemaker living room had begun to speak of relatives who'd passed on. Sylvia was seated on the floor looking up at Ada when slowly the form of a man, standing at Grandma's shoulder, began to take shape. At first he was merely a filmy outline, but then he grew clearer and clearer until he was as distinct as Ada.

"Who's that man behind you, Grandma?" the child asked.

"Just Sylvia showing off" was the consensus of the group—except for Ada, who asked matter-of-factly, "What does he look like?"

"He's tall with reddish brown hair. He has a nice face with little wire glasses."

"Anything else?"

"Well, he's wearing a string around his neck with a horn on it."

"A horn?"

"Yes, he listens to people's chests with it."

"Could it be Jim?" Celeste ventured.

"Of course, it must be," Ada agreed. "You're looking at your Uncle Jim," she explained to Sylvia. "He died in the flu epidemic of 1917. He caught it from one of his patients."

That experience was a pleasant one, with Sylvia sitting

on Ada's lap and hearing about the things that Uncle Jim had done as a child. But most of the time Sylvia was very much alone. She knew without being told that none of her friends experienced the struggles that frequently beset her; she could scarcely define them herself. In crowds, the child would suffer bouts of severe exhaustion that frequently led to depression. It was years before she would learn to "turn off" the disturbing incubi of those about her.

But those occasions weren't always burdensome or negative. Once, while attending a movie with her father, Sylvia suddenly began to hyperventilate. Both she and Bill were enjoying the comedy immensely, and the seven-year-old tried to overcome the sensation. But its intensity only increased. A sick dizziness swept over her. The panic was overwhelming. Am I dying? she thought wildly. "No," a voice inside replied, "someone else."

Frantically the frightened child tried to remain calm, tried to resist the waves of sickening panic. Where is this coming from? she asked herself.

Seemingly in answer, a picture flashed before her mind's eye, clear and bold as the one on the screen—her baby sister gasping for air. "We've got to go," Sylvia whispered to her father. "There's something terribly the matter with Sharon. She can't breathe. She's turning blue."

"That's ridiculous," he chided her. "We just left Sharon an hour ago. She's fine."

But Sylvia, now desperately frightened, persisted. Sharon's life depended on Bill believing her. "Daddy, we have to go home *now*," she ended with a scream.

"You'd better know what you're talking about," Bill snapped, as the two of them picked their way between the seats of the darkened theater, stumbling over the feet of the annoyed spectators around them.

The ride home was an agony for Sylvia, who was now experiencing all of Sharon's symptoms. "Hurry, Daddy, hurry," she pleaded. Her lungs seemed to be bursting with the effort to breathe. Certain that her sister must be dying, she gasped frantically for air. It seemed an eternity had passed when the frightened child at last saw her house in the distance.

As their car turned into the drive, Celeste ran out sobbing. The phone was out of order. Sharon had become desperately ill with what turned out to be double pneumonia. Bill was just in time to rush the infant to the hospital.

Grateful as they were for this apparent miracle, it was obscured by Sylvia's eccentricity, which Bill and Celeste saw increasing every day. She wasn't an easy child for them to understand. Their lives were complicated enough without the aberration of this "strange" little creature who tuned in psychically to every family secret and insisted on pointing out ghosts.

Sylvia's double vision was becoming a nuisance. The otherworldly dimension that had crept unbidden into their life was a nighttime distraction. "It's like a parade of people walking back and forth in my room," she attempted to explain. "Give her a flashlight," Grandma Ada advised.

One night, a few months after the incident of Sharon's illness, Sylvia was shining the light along the wall. Suddenly, it began to expand until it filled the entire room. Out of nowhere a tall, dark-haired woman appeared. She smiled and said, "Dear Sylvia, don't be afraid, I come from God."

The words signaled yet another psychic "gift." At eight, Sylvia had become clairaudient. Now, besides seeing things that others didn't see, Sylvia heard voices they didn't hear.

It's true that—as in the vision of the free-flying birds—there had been auditory sensations almost like whispered thoughts. But these words were spoken clearly and directly into Sylvia's ears. Don't be afraid, indeed! The child fled, shrieking, from the room.

Ada Coil put her arms around the screaming child. "It's just a bad dream," she explained to Celeste and Bill, who regarded their daughter with bewildered dismay. Gently, she led Sylvia up the stairs to the guest room.

Between sobs that gradually turned to hiccoughs, the frightened little girl explained what had happened. "Oh, is that all? I've heard voices all my life," Ada reassured her. "You've just made contact with your spirit guide—someone like a guardian angel, a person who's there to help you. You can be happy—not frightened. Most people never meet their guides."

Dear Grandma, the pillar of Sylvia's family, of her entire world! If *she* heard voices, perhaps it was okay. Sylvia stopped crying and began to listen. The appearance of a spirit guide was the beginning of what was to become the strongest, most enduring relationship of her life. Yet in those early days the friendship was an uneasy one. Often, when the now-familiar buzz and high-pitched whine started, signaling the beginning of a message, the child would panic, almost paralyzed by terror. At the same time, she was filled with curiosity and a sense of destiny.

Iena, Sylvia's quide, took a lot of getting used to. The name alone was a bit off-putting. At the time, Francine was Sylvia's favorite name ("Oh, Mom, if only you'd named me Francine instead of dumb old Sylvia") so that's what the child rechristened her new companion. "Lots of children have made-up friends," Celeste and Bill, still resisting, reminded one another in the beginning. But as time passed and Francine's predictions, imparted to them by Sylvia, came true, they ruefully began to revise their opinions.

Sylvia saw no conflict between Francine's ever-increasing presence and the teachings of the nuns. Weren't they forever talking of guardian angels and messages from God? Maybe she wasn't so different, after all. The thought brought Sylvia some relief from her family's accelerating chaos.

Bill's fortunes were improving. From mailman, he'd progressed to jewelry salesman, then to employment with a major freight line, where he would eventually rise to vice president. He was sexually aggressive as well—warmly humorous, dashing, debonair, Bill had no difficulty finding partners. Again and again the Shoemakers teetered on the brink of divorce.

During a brief period of unity, Bill and Celeste begged and borrowed their way into possession of a three-story Victorian mansion. The purchase was meant as a promise of a future of affluence and solidarity. The solidarity, however, was never to materialize.

After enduring the many moves linked with her father's financial successes and amatory weaknesses, Sylvia perceived the new home as a bastion. She loved it and knew in her heart that the house loved her as well. Running from room to room, she took a delighted inventory: An impressive entry with large walnut pillars and graceful stairway, an inviting living room accented by a tile fireplace, an elegant dining room with stained glass windows, a large, homey kitchen and butler's pantry, four large bedrooms, and, finally, the promising mystery of an attic to explore.

The Shoemakers moved in—Bill and Celeste, Sylvia and Sharon. Happily for Sylvia, Grandma Ada came too and along with her came "Brother." Sylvia adored her uncle, a lifelong invalid. Despite a crippling birth defect accompanied by a form of vertigo that caused his head to be pulled to one side, Brother had a brilliant mind and a sweet and gentle disposition. Grandma cared for him lovingly and protectively; Sylvia kept him entertained with lively chatter. On one occasion, Brother may have saved his niece's life.

Sylvia had been sitting in the front yard when, for no apparent reason, she became aware of a sudden, anxious sensation. Today the psychic recognizes that visceral feeling as a warning of imminent danger. She stood still, puzzled, unsure of what to do next.

"Run!" a voice called out. Looking up, Sylvia saw Brother emerge from the house walking much faster than anyone thought he could. "Run, run, run!" he yelled to his niece.

Sylvia froze. Run where? What was happening? She sat motionless, literally paralyzed with fear. And then she saw what Brother had seen. It was a figure out of a nightmare. Racing toward her was a large woman with unkempt hair and wild black eyes. Her face, so pale that it appeared stark white, was contorted in an expression of pure hatred. It seemed to the terrified child that time had slowed almost to a standstill. This fearful creature was lumbering toward her in slow but inexorable motion.

"Run, Sylvia, run!"

Somehow, she never knew how, Sylvia moved out of the way just as frail, little Brother interposed himself and took the full brunt of the woman's crazed frenzy. She knocked him to the ground and was fiercely pummeling him with her fists when two more women who appeared at the sound of Sylvia's frightened screams managed to pull her away. The effort took all their combined strength.

Later it was learned that the attacker was the mentally disturbed daughter of a wealthy neighbor who kept her at home under the questionable protection of two psychiatric nurses rather than institutionalize her.

Delightful as the house was, the family scene wasn't enough for Bill. Or perhaps it was too much. Whatever the cause, it wasn't long after the move that he became involved in yet another romance, this one more significant. A compromise was reached. Bill would remain married while settling his mistress into a comfortable apartment conveniently located six blocks from home.

Despite all the distractions, he remained a devoted father. Bill doted on Sylvia but set high standards for her. "Show them what you can do" was his favorite refrain. Fearful that she, like her mother, might lose the attention of this mercurial man, Sylvia determined not to disappoint him. What if some random act on her part inadvertantly drove her father away forever? She must never do anything to cause dissension; it was her duty to please everyone. The responsibility was overwhelming.

But her increasing acceptance of her psychic gifts compensated and Sylvia's natural vivacity returned. Great things were expected of this quick, witty child. This was the era of Shirley Temple clones and Sylvia seemed a natural. She was enrolled in dancing school, but as the family watched the row of little girls in abbreviated sailor suits tapping obediently to the tune of *Anchors Aweigh*, it became obvious that whatever her other gifts, the one talent their daughter lacked was coordination.

Her stamina and determination were never in question. "Wait till you see me do *Singing in the Rain*, Daddy," she promised. On the day of her first recital, as she rushed eagerly on stage, virtually attacking it, she caught her umbrella on a stage prop. It pulled inside out but the plucky child pranced out undismayed, clutching the shattered umbrella valiantly as she struggled with the step. *Dark Eyes*, her final number, was a true showstopper. While dancing about the gypsy circle, Sylvia created a sensation by stumbling into the canned fire. Glancing down in dismay, she realized what she'd done, but quickly forced a determined smile and danced back into the fire, hoping by her air of cheery abandon to convince the audience that it was all part of the act. Her memory of the occasion is of looking anxiously out over the crowd and spotting her father, head buried in his hands.

Sylvia's whole life became one of performance, of dedication. She was determined to please, to entertain, and to soothe. Her efforts and the self-discipline she had to learn served as a kind of conditioning. It was as though she was a young athlete training for the big meet.

Late one night, while lying sleepless, Sylvia was startled by the vision of two masks superimposed on the wall before her—the classical Greek comedy and tragedy masks. Their significance was explained by Francine, who told her, "Sylvia, this is your life."

The words were prophetic. Death and its many implications—reincarnation, mediumship, documentation of soul survival—play a daily part in her life. And so does comedy. Anyone who's ever watched Sylvia Brown on stage or television has witnessed a superb comedienne at work. Humor is the spoonful of sugar that enables us to laugh at the dark mysteries of life and death. Without it and its comedic corollary the psychic lacks humanity.

As time passed, Francine made herself increasingly visible. She's an imposing figure, an Indian woman standing five feet, six inches, slender with long black hair and brown, almond-shaped eyes. She speaks simply and precisely, conveying much in just a few words. Her message has always been one of tolerance, compassion, and forgiveness, her direct approach both modest and practical.

In the beginning, she talked with Sylvia about things a child would respond to. At first the little girl was primarily interested in games. It was amusing to Sylvia to repeat to the family conversations that she couldn't possibly have overheard. The surprised reaction was instant validation and it further reinforced the confidence of the young medium.

As their friendship grew, Sylvia asked Francine questions about herself. Iena/Francine had been born in northern Colombia in the year 1500. She identified herself as an Aztec/Inca, a term that would later confuse many. Francine explained that though Hunayna Capac, the Inca ruler, was dominant, the influence of Montezuma, far to the north, was also felt by her people. There was much communication between the two cultures—a blending that is only now being verified by archaeologists.

Sylvia was fascinated with Francine's childhood, her teachers' training, and her betrothal at the age of sixteen to a young silversmith. When Francine was eighteen she was married and within a year a baby girl was born. Sylvia often pictured the large open-air market which adjoined the emperor's vast grounds, where Francine went often with her toddler daughter to sell her husband's wares. It was here that a runner from an outlying village came one day to warn of strangers who'd invaded their land. It wasn't long before the Spaniards arrived to plunder the city. Hundreds of Indians were murdered and Francine was among them. She was impaled by a spear while trying to protect her child.

This was, Francine told Sylvia, her one and only life on this earth. Though she had but one goal—to help people—she had no wish to return to the world as a mortal. From 1520 until Sylvia's birth in 1936, she had worked on the other side to facilitate the transitions of those who died through war or other violence. She and Sylvia were close friends in the spirit world and made a pact that they would work together as guide and subject in Sylvia's next incarnation on earth.

Despite her powers, Sylvia had no memory of any of this. It was necessary for Francine to explain it in a manner that a child could understand. There's nothing mysterious about a spirit guide, Francine said. A guide is very much like a human except that he or she resides on the other side. The guide's job is to help a given individual through the present incarnation. Most everyone on earth has been or will be a spiritual guide for someone.

The spirit guide's purpose is to research, suggest, nudge,

and encourage the person whom he or she may be guiding through life. In most cases the guides operate in the individual's subconscious, appearing as the "voice of conscience." They will illustrate lessons and speak of what the individual is here to learn, but they never interfere with choices. They are extremely careful never to preclude the opportunity for a person to learn a life lesson. If the subject is headed toward an event that will teach a valuable but difficult lesson, a guide may point out an alternative route. The decision remains with the individual; if that choice involves pain and struggle the guide won't prevent it.

According to Francine, spirit guides may use a variety of methods to communicate. They convey knowledge through dreams, or as a flash in the mind's eye, even occasionally as a voice. It's a frustrating task, Francine told Sylvia, because few people take time to really listen.

As Sylvia was growing up, Francine was a constant adviser and companion, slowly and carefully imparting the wisdom that would become the medium's philosophy. "Some day you will be a great psychic," Francine informed Sylvia. "You will help many people and will be asked to speak before large groups of people."

Remembering her failed career as a dancer, Sylvia was anything but pleased by the prospect. Seeking comfort from her grandmother, she pleaded, "I don't have to do that if I don't want to, do I?"

Ada patted the little girl reassuringly. "Of course not, but when the time comes and you're ready, you'll be able to do it."

But the shy little girl would grow into an audacious, spirited woman. The time would soon come when Sylvia would seek a life of her own.

The spirit would warn, but the woman would not hear the message.

CHAPTER THREE

A Psychic in Love

JOE studied Sylvia intently, admiring the woman, remembering the girl. In many ways they were much the same. She'd always been special. The warmth, the humor, the enthusiasm, and yes, the sex appeal.

It was obvious to this out-of-town visitor touring the impressive offices of the Nirvana Foundation that Sylvia Shoemaker was a long way from Kansas City. "What was it like growing up with Sylvia?" one of her staff asked him.

Joe paused, thinking back over a friendship that had begun when they were children more than forty years before. "No big deal," he replied at last, "although we always seemed to be waiting for her to tell us what was going to happen next."

Sylvia smiled, recalling many such times. Joe turned back to her. "Do you still have that lady talking into your ear, telling you things?"

"Yes, Francine's around. I don't think she'll check out until I do."

He watched her, still searching for traces of the impetuous but vulnerable friend he remembered. "Are you happy in California? Do they treat you right here?"

"Yes—yes, I'm really very happy," she assured him.

"You know you can always come home. We take care of our own in Missouri," he reminded her.

"Protect me like the village idiot? That's comforting," she teased him, amused, but also warmed by memories of the past. It seemed in retrospect that the Kansas City of her childhood had been frozen in time. Families stayed in place, neighborhoods remained unchanged. Everyone knew everyone, everyone knew *everything* about everyone—and before long they took it all for granted. Without realizing it at the time, Sylvia had been provided with the perfect shelter, the shelter so sorely needed by a psychic.

She'd done her first psychic reading at age eight. It had happened spontaneously when a friend named Mary Marguerite had complained. "What shall I do about my mother? She's getting so cranky."

"I don't know about that, but I *can* see your mother falling down and breaking her arm." Though Sylvia had always known things, this was the first time anyone had deliberately sought information from her. Her inadvertent response to Mary Marguerite's question had somehow revealed her psychic insight. She could actually ask her spirit guide a question and have it answered. "Your mother's going to break her arm!" she repeated, amazed at herself. Then she added, "Your father—I see him too. He's going to lose his job."

Mary Marguerite accepted the news matter-of-factly, not nearly as surprised as Sylvia. Since she'd known since toddler days that her friend was a bit different, this new development didn't appear particularly remarkable. "What about me?" she asked. "Is anything bad going to happen to me?"

"No—well, a little bad. You're going to slip and fall on the ice. Don't be afraid. You won't break anything."

Mary Marguerite nodded, then went on to chatter about other things. It was the same Mary Marguerite—by then calling herself Maggie—who Sylvia would overhear ten years later attempting to explain Sylvia's strangeness to two visitors from a nearby men's college. "Sylvia might *seem* a little different—sometimes she knows things before they happen—but she's really lots of fun. She's just like anyone except for that."

The "Sylvia's one of us" attitude of her friends, possibly fostered by her own down-to-earth exuberance and humor, has accompanied the psychic all her life. The conflicts and challenges that have beset Sylvia are numerous and varied; but in this one area, she has remained truly fortunate. She grew up with the same group of boys and girls, attended school with them for twelve years, and continued with many of them at St. Theresa's College. Although her psychic gifts and tensions might have set her apart, the affection, support, and casual acceptance of lifelong friends formed a protective shield to her vulnerability.

"What about you, Joe?" Sylvia asked, her eyes returning to the man who still watched her thoughtfully. "I hear you married four times. Which wife was your favorite?"

"That's easy. The first."

Sylvia's eyes filled as she thought of that long-ago marriage, their marriage. She'd been sixteen when her father announced that he'd at last met the woman he couldn't live without. Stormy threats of divorce and tearful attempts at reconciliation were all she'd ever known from her parents. Now Celeste and Bill really had something to quarrel over—their children. Being placed in the middle of a custody battle was agony to a girl whose entire young life had been devoted to pleasing everyone. How could she possibly choose to live with one parent at the expense of the other? Sylvia was literally ill from the rage and fear she absorbed psychically from both parents.

At this period in her life, Sharon was a shy, introverted child who clung to her mother for support. She would live with Celeste, of course. But what about Sylvia? Probing psychically, she saw herself being sent to live with her mother as well. The sense of Bill's pain, his loneliness and desolation, was overwhelming.

Then, while sitting in algebra class, the answer came to her: Joe Tschirhart. If she married him, the decision of which parent to live with would be moot. Of course, her other boyfriend, Warren Becker would be disappointed, but hurting her father or mother would be far worse.

Joe was easy to convince. How could he resist when Sylvia explained that he was the only one who could help her with this terrible problem? Besides, he'd hoped to marry her anyway—some day. That night, Sylvia located her birth certificate and altered it so that her age read eighteen. The following day after school, the two teen-agers took a streetcar across the state line to the other Kansas City.

The enormity of it all engulfed Sylvia as she stood before the justice of the peace. Had she really signed her whole life away to this boy beside her? She was a Catholic girl; marriage was forever. A giant wave of homesickness swept over her at the thought of what she'd done. Sylvia had just been pronounced a wife and all she wanted was to be her parents' little girl.

"What about our honeymoon?" Joe had asked, survey-ing his bride, who'd selected a white pinafore with match-ing bobbysox and oxfords for the occasion. "It's Friday and we've got two days before we have to go back to school."

"I don't think my parents would like it," Sylvia de-murred. "Let's just keep it our secret for a while."

Joe wasn't entirely disappointed. He had his own par-ents to contend with. Agreeably, he'd taken Sylvia home, settling for a quick but ardent kiss before leaving her on the doorstep.

Celeste was waiting in the living room, her eyes on the clock. "Where have you been?" was her first question. "What's that bulge under your dress?" was the second.

Sylvia looked down at the telltale bulge. Why had she been so careless? Of course she had to tell her parents sometime; that was the whole point of the runaway marriage. But not now. She wasn't ready. Would she ever be ready? The runaway marriage that had seemed like such a grand and daring solution was obviously a disaster. Sylvia felt sick with remorse. Her hand strayed to the front of her pinafore, trying to push it down. "Oh, just a license," she murmured.

"License! License to what, for God's sake?" Celeste yelled as Sylvia fled sobbing up the stairs. Mrs. Shoemaker retired with unprecedented urgency to her bath as Bill pounded on their daughter's door demanding to be admitted.

"You can't come in, Daddy, I'm a married woman. I'm in charge of my life now," Sylvia announced in a quavering voice.

Not yet, she wasn't. To Sylvia's immense, but secret, relief, Bill had the marriage annulled in record time. Unfortunately, there was nothing that he could do to prevent the appearance of the wedding announcement in the vital statistics column of the newspaper.

The punishment agreed upon by both sets of parents was that Joe and Sylvia would refrain from seeing one another socially. The romance was over before it began.

Grandma Ada came to the rescue as she had so many times before. "What are we going to do with Sylvia?" Celeste demanded of her.

"What are we going to do with *you*?" had been the answer. As a result of Ada's firm but tactful mediation, a compromise was reached once again and life continued at the Shoemakers.

After a few months Joe Behm came along and filled the void in Sylvia's affections. This Joe was a bit older. His formal education completed, he had a good job with a trucking firm and felt ready for marriage. Sylvia, too, was maturing; her elopement and its embarrassing aftermath had been a crash course in reality. Joe talked of a farm and six children. To Sylvia, with her growing need for security, it sounded wonderful. But there was one major drawback. Joe was a possessive young man and he wanted Sylvia all to himself—no sharing her with the spirit world. Joe was threatened by the small measure of notoriety that Sylvia's psychic gifts had brought. When Sylvia was "on," Joe was very uncomfortable.

"Either Francine goes or I do," he told her, and he meant it.

Sylvia was torn. She loved Joe—or thought she did—and fantasized about the life they might have together. Her dreams of becoming a teacher, maybe even a teaching nun, dated from early childhood. But she'd recently begun to reconsider. Would having children of her own be even more satisfying? She pondered the question endlessly.

Many of Sylvia's friends planned to marry soon after high school. There was a seductive sense of independence about the idea of having one's own home, one's own family. Sylvia viewed marriage as romantic and simple, easily ignoring the tumultuous relationship of her parents. The idea of a tranquil, uncomplicated life with a very solid young man who adored her was highly appealing.

For once, neither Grandma Ada nor Francine were of help. Francine, despite her life on earth as an Indian woman, was amazingly liberated. For all her supernatural powers, she refused to take seriously the pressures of an era that introduced the family room and delighted in *I Love Lucy*. By Francine's otherworldly standards, the child-centered, family-oriented decade that marked Sylvia's transition from girl to woman was merely a temporary aberration.

Grandma Ada hoped so too, but lacked a discarnate spirit's concept of time. Years were years to her—not instants, as they are to Francine. Somehow, Ada realized, Sylvia must come to terms with *this* world, yet the destiny she perceived for her granddaughter was a far cry from the craze for domesticity that was sweeping the country.

Ada had seen women function brilliantly during two world wars; she remembered the independent New Woman of the 1920s and the strong dominant females called forth by the Great Depression. Now, surveying the young women of the 1950s with their cinched waists, voluminous skirts, and multiple petticoats, she realized that most of them regarded careers as mere time-passers to be readily abandoned when the right man came along. Although Joe *had* come along a little early, who was to say that this serious-minded young man wasn't just the thing for Sylvia? "Wait," was all that Ada could or would say. "When the time comes, you'll know the right thing to do."

As her high school years drew to a close, Sylvia realized that her adored grandmother was having serious problems of her own. She had a critical heart condition. An attack, the doctors said, would certainly be fatal. Ada had listened calmly to the diagnosis, accepting the death sentence implicit in the warning with equanimity. To her, death as we know it was merely "going home." Why should anyone fear that? Her only concern was Brother. "I can't leave this world without him," she told Sylvia. "No one can ever understand and care for him the way I have."

"But you're not going anywhere, Grandma," Sylvia insisted, hoping desperately that the very intensity of her desire could somehow make the words come true.

She was eighteen and a college freshman when the call came that Ada had been hospitalized. "Your grandmother wants you to have this," a nurse said, handing Sylvia a black crucifix. Ada was enclosed in an oxygen tent, her eyes shut.

"Grandma, you have to get well. I love you," Sylvia said as she knelt beside the fragile body.

Ada said nothing, but her china-blue eyes opened briefly. "*Go on, Sylvia.*" The words were never spoken but the sobbing girl heard them as clearly as if they'd been shouted.

Sylvia sat for hours beside her sleeping grandmother. It was late evening before she returned home. There was a light on in Brother's room. Pulling a chair up beside his bed, Sylvia sank down wearily. Taking the crucifix from her purse, she offered it to him. "This should really be yours."

Brother shook his head. "You keep it, Syl. I don't think I'll need it now." The two, each seeking solace and finding some measure of comfort in their shared grief, said the Rosary together as they had so many times during Sylvia's growing-up years.

The next day Sylvia returned to the hospital and began a vigil that would last several days. She was seated alone at Ada's side when her grandmother died. Celeste was home in her bathtub. Two days later, returning from her grandmother's memorial service, Sylvia paused in the doorway of Brother's room. "Grandmother looked beautiful," she started to say, then stopped. Her uncle was having convulsions.

Brother was rushed to the hospital. He died two hours later. The autopsy report read "cause unknown." Equally baffling were the stacks of neatly folded clothing discovered that night in Brother's room—he'd never folded an article of clothing in his life. His affairs in order—papers carefully stacked beside the garments, Brother had died before Ada was even in the ground.

In the days that followed, Joe Behm was constantly at Sylvia's side, offering love and support. "Why not quit college now? What's the point? We'll just be getting married when you graduate anyway," he urged. Bill, admiring the young man's progress in the trucking line, had come to agree. "You don't need college to be a wife and mother," he told his daughter. Celeste was vague. "Do what you want most, hon," was her only advice.

Francine remained adamant. "You'll need this training," she insisted. "You will need your college education for the work that you will do. Teaching will be a part of it."

But Sylvia was seeing less and less of Francine, trying with increasing success to exclude her spirit guide. To please Joe, she'd stopped doing readings. Though Francine never totally disappeared, she was no longer a part of Sylvia's life. Her wisdom and companionship were withdrawn. Bereft, Sylvia studied the woman in her family—her role models. Each invariably placed the wishes of her man above everything. Joe wanted a traditional "all-around girl" and that's what Sylvia tried desperately to be. Gone was the exhilaration of the readings, the sense of satisfaction from helping, and the psychic attunement to the entity who had been her dearest friend. Years later, Sylvia would remember what this soul-wracking effort had cost. Her body, weary of the battle within, was vulnerable to everything. Without understanding the cause, she suffered almost serial illnesses: persistent colds, flu, bronchitis, pneumonia.

Joe continued his efforts to persuade Sylvia to drop out of college, but as the months passed an exciting new world opened up, exerting a powerful claim of its own. Despite her myriad health problems, Sylvia was enjoying college more and more, and soon would not hear of abandoning it. She was majoring in both education and literature with a minor in theology. Her old desire to teach had returned full force, yet a part of her still craved the security she believed came only from marriage. Now it appeared that, although she'd tried with some success to exorcise the paranormal side of her life, she still lived in two worlds. One was college life—late nights spent in philosophical and metaphysical discussions on Huxley, Kafka, Camus, Sartre, Bertrand Russell, and Alan Watts. The other world was the "real" one inhabited by Joe and the solid, home-centered life she envisioned with him.

With the exception of Joe's reservations about her

paranormal life, he was an easy man to be around. He adored Sylvia and accepted her uncritically. Remembering his quiet strength during the bleak months following Ada's death, Sylvia felt certain that Joe would be a fine husband and father. As graduation approached, the pressure to make a decision increased. "That young man won't wait around forever," Bill warned. "He's too good a guy to let slip away," her girlfriends cautioned. Added to this was the longing that Sylvia read in Joe's eyes. She could feel the pain her reluctance was causing him. For a young woman whose whole life had been centered about pleasing others, this was the worst part.

Finally, in her senior year, Sylvia agreed to the marriage. Having at last made a decision, she felt immense relief. Whether it was the right one or not scarcely mattered; a weight had been lifted from her. Now she allowed herself to be swept into a flurry of preparations for a June wedding. Joe made a down payment on a house and the couple were in the process of selecting furniture when again fate intervened.

Business, not philosophy, was Joe's forté. Though only a few years older than Sylvia's college friends, he sometimes felt out of place with them and rarely attended the parties she gave nearly every week. Sylvia has always wondered how her life might have differed had he been present that cold, winter evening when someone new walked in.

"Meet my rescuer," Maggie announced dramatically. "I was stuck in the snow and—"

Sylvia didn't hear the rest. She was staring into the greenest, the most compelling eyes she'd ever seen. His smile, the force of his almost animal magnetism literally took her breath away. *"Tragedy, Sylvia!"* The words were sharp and clear, a kind of psychic telegram from Francine, who'd remained in the background for the past two years. It was the first time in months that she had communicated.

"This is the beginning of the most difficult time of your life."

Alarming the message was, but Sylvia was nineteen and looking into the eyes of her first true love—a tall, dark stranger.

"I'm the hostess with the mostest," she introduced herself with the glibness that came so easily to her, but that disguised her vulnerability.

"I can see that."

He moved his rangy body with a graceful ease that reminded Sylvia of a panther. She found it immensely attractive. Everything about him was attractive—even the broken nose that Sylvia thought very masculine. All evening Sylvia could feel his eyes on her until finally she could stand the mounting tension no longer. "Why do you keep staring?" she asked him.

"Because I have big eyes for you."

To a romantic teenager it was movie dialogue; here, obviously attracted to her, was a man as handsome as any star. She felt dizzy with excitement. It was a moment out of every romantic novel she'd ever read and now it was actually happening to her. As the party drew to a close and guests gathered to take their leave, the stranger swept Sylvia into his arms for a long, lingering kiss. Bantering farewells halted abruptly. Who was this older man who'd barged into a private party and was making time with one of the most popular girls on campus?

He was yet another Joe—Joseph Stemkowski, but Sylvia quickly named him "Ski." That evening, almost at the moment of their meeting, her engagement to Joe Behm ended. Sylvia would tell him in the morning. For her, suddenly, passionately aware of the reality of love, it was as though their four-year relationship had never been.

Ski was slightly mysterious; new in town, he'd come from New Jersey to study flight engineering. Dazzled by his good looks and charm, swept away by the force of their mutual attraction, Sylvia spent every possible moment with him. She was happier than she'd ever been before, but bewildered too. Hidden behind the excitement was a nagging feeling that something wasn't quite right. It was as if, in Ski, Sylvia had found the other half of herself. It was ecstatic, yet just beyond the radiance there were shadows. Try as she might, Sylvia could neither dispel nor penetrate them.

Released from the strictures imposed by Joe Behm, she resumed her readings. She received all sorts of information for others, but none for herself. "What did you mean by tragedy?" she asked Francine again and again. "If there's something I should know, tell me," she pleaded. But after her initial warning, Francine remained curiously silent on the subject of Ski.

Then one afternoon Sylvia encountered another engineering student, a friend of Ski's. They chatted amiably about trivialities, while Sylvia debated quizzing him. If anything was wrong, did she really want to know? At last she forced herself to probe for the answers that had eluded her psychically. "Ski's wonderful, but why do I feel that something's terribly wrong?"

He looked away, uncertain, avoiding her eyes. "Aren't you the one who's supposed to know everything? Don't you have that lady in your head who tells you stuff?"

"Not about me. I've never gotten any help from her with my own personal life—nothing about the future," Sylvia explained. "It never mattered much until now. Francine always said when the time came I'd know what I needed to know. Now she doesn't say anything and I sense there's something I need to find out."

"Well, there is," he admitted after a long pause. "Ski's married. He's got a wife back in New Jersey. A wife and two kids."

In that instant the world grew dark and dirty. Sylvia was

suddenly conscious of grime everywhere. Tattered papers blowing in the street, littered gutters. The sun had vanished for her. I'm going to have to live my whole life in twilight, she thought. A Catholic girl, a married man; it was impossible. She drove to the flight school, determined to confront Ski. Perhaps there was a mistake, Sylvia reasoned, but she knew there wasn't. Ski knew the moment he saw her. "It was only a matter of time before you found out," he said dully.

"Why didn't you tell me yourself?"

"I didn't want to lose you."

Sylvia nodded. Unbidden, a picture of a dark-haired woman with a small boy and girl appeared before her.

He attempted to explain. "I was very young, a sailor away from home for the first time. She got pregnant. I had to marry her, but I really tried to make it work. It never did. That's why I came to Kansas City to study. I thought distance would give me some perspective. I never dreamed I'd meet someone like you, God knows. I never meant for it to happen."

Sylvia felt a wave of pain and guilt as she thought of Joe Behm. This terrible emptiness must be what he experienced. It was as if she'd aged twenty years in an instant. What a callous child she'd been. Life in that perpetual twilight, deprived forever of the warmth that was Ski, seemed a just punishment for her thoughtlessness, her cruelty. But how could she survive it?

"Will you see me tonight—one last night?" Ski pleaded.

Sylvia nodded, unable to speak. Two weeks passed, each night "the last one." The two were more in love than ever, a frantic, devouring kind of love. Then one afternoon a messenger came to Sylvia's French class. Father Nadeux wanted to see her immediately in his office.

Sylvia had taken theology and Christian marriage classes from the Dominican priest. Once, in an impish mood, she'd scrawled, "Don't let this lead you into false conceptions," in a textbook written by the teacher—knowing all the while that he was watching. Father Nadeux had been more amused than annoyed. Since then, Sylvia had often been singled out for special praise or encouragement by the portly, good-natured man.

Entering his high-beamed study, she mentally reviewed her school conduct. Since Ski had come into her life, the pranks that had marked her college career had ceased. What could she have done this time?

Father Nadeux didn't keep her long in suspense. She'd scarcely seated herself before he began. "I have a letter from a Mrs. Joseph Stemkowski. Someone has informed her of her husband's involvement with one of our girls. Do you have any idea who it might be?"

"It's I, Father."

He turned away, looking absently out at the spring landscape—tender green shoots of life everywhere. "Do you love him?"

"Oh, yes, more than anything in the world."

Sighing, he turned back to face her. "That makes it more difficult. You know, of course, what you must do."

"Father, I can't give him up. I've tried, but I can't."

"You must, Sylvia. You know that." The priest knew her well. "You'll find the strength to do what has to be done."

His words echoed eerily. Sylvia could hear Grandma Ada not long before her death saying, "Within your weakness, there lies your strength sleeping." What did *that* mean? Grandma, she screamed inwardly. Where are you? Explain it to me, help me!

Sylvia left the room without another word. Somewhere, nuns were chanting, "Lord have mercy, Lord have mercy." What could they know? she thought bitterly. None of them could ever have had anyone like Ski in their lives, anyone so handsome and humorous, tender and poetic. Loving him was an addiction. He'd made her feel like a woman, the most beautiful, desirable woman in the world. How could she give that up? Could anyone hurt as much as she did and not die from it?

"For every hurt there is a reason—a reason to grow and to understand." The words were there suddenly, a response from Francine, but what good could they do? Francine's life on this earth was over, her own just beginning. The years ahead stretched before Sylvia, an empty wasteland.

She waved her hand over her right shoulder in a gesture used since childhood to dismiss Francine. "I'm tired of your spirit world platitudes. Go talk to someone else."

"They won't hear me."

"Because they're not crazy."

"Don't start that 'crazy' notion again."

"Do you know any sane people who have spirits talking to them?"

"You always ask that when you're overwrought."

"Overwrought! I want to die!"

"You won't," Francine said and then was silent. The internal dialogue had ended.

At home later that afternoon, Sylvia did call Ski. She told him about the letter and described her conversation with Father Nadeux.

"I've got to see you," he pleaded.

"No, no more. Never again," she forced herself to say and then hung up before he could reply.

Sylvia refused to take Ski's calls, fearing the effect of his voice on her shaky resolve. On the third day, a nun summoned her from class. "You know it's against the rules," she reminded Sylvia, "but since your cousin is on his way to Korea and will only be in town a few hours, I decided to bend the rules." Ski was standing behind her in the hall, pale-faced, hollow-eyed.

"No one will believe this," Sylvia said as the nun departed. "She's the one we call Old Ironsides. You must have really charmed her."

"Maybe she sensed how desperate I am. I had to see you. School's over. I have to decide what to do—stay here or go back."

"You know the answer to that," she said, pushing him from her with all her force and running back into the classroom.

There was one last call from Ski. Celeste had answered the phone. After listening to his message, she handed the receiver to Sylvia. "I think you'll want to take this call," she said. The following evening Sylvia drove Ski to the bus station. "When this life's over, I'll meet you on the second star to the right," he said, getting out of the car.

"It's a date," Sylvia replied, trying to smile.

"Maybe if this reconciliation doesn't work out, I can—"

She shook her head. Failed promises were scattered about them like punctured balloons. It was no use. They had had five months together. Sylvia knew it was all they'd ever have. Perhaps Ski knew it too, and perhaps on some level he knew even more.

Just before he boarded the bus, he turned to Sylvia and said, "Write to the Browns."

"What?" she exclaimed in surprise. "What Brown? Who do you mean?"

"I don't know," he answered, looking at her in bewilderment. "It just came into my head. It must be from a song or something." Then he was on the bus, the last passenger to board.

The engine started, slowly the bus began to pull out. Sylvia moved forward. Ski was trying to get the window open, but it was stuck. Sylvia was running now, trying to keep up. Ski finally got the window open, and she reached up, touching his face with her fingers. Ski kissed her palm; she could feel his tears.

It was June. Sylvia was nineteen. Within a week she would graduate from college, but her world had ended.

Create a void and something invariably fills it. As if Ski's departure were not enough, Sylvia seemed almost to be seeking an acceleration of her pain. Perhaps it was a secret wish for punishment, a need to flagellate herself still further for real or imagined sins. Or possibly it was a perverse desire to enkindle deadened senses. Whatever the latent cause, Sylvia's excoriation took the form of fear. College classes in abnormal psychology had opened a Pandora's box of doubts. According to the textbooks, there were seven levels of abnormal behavior. Sylvia fit at least four. Her agile mind leaped to the worst possible conclusion.

She was a schizophrenic. After all, those struck with the disorder heard voices and saw visions. She was haunted by memories of the crazed neighbor who'd tried to kill her as a child. Again and again, she pictured Brother's battered, bloody body. How could a potential maniac even consider working with children?

Earlier, diverted by Joe and his constant talk of marriage and later by her passionate romance with Ski, Sylvia had been able to push those ugly thoughts from her mind. Now, with her whole being focused on teaching, her doubts virtually paralyzed her.

Teaching had always been natural for Sylvia. From earliest childhood, her favorite toy had been a small blackboard and chalk. Playing school was a cherished memory. She'd delighted in "teaching" anyone she could corral. When she'd entered college there'd never been a question of what she would study. And, as in her paranormal life, Grandma Ada had encouraged her. "You will be a fine teacher, Sylvia, an inspiration," she said many times. Unfortunately by the time Sylvia had reached her abormal psychology class, Ada was gone.

"How can I teach children when I might be crazy?" she asked almost frantically of anyone who would listen. No one took her seriously. "Of course you're not crazy," Sylvia's young women friends would invariably respond, surprised that she'd even consider the possibility. Then they'd change the subject to their love lives. "What does Francine say about Dave?" they would ask, or "There's this new guy . . ." Celeste and Bill, occupied as usual with their ongoing drama, would nod absently, assuring Sylvia that she was perfectly sane and suggesting that she forget teaching for a year and just have fun. Then they would go back to their bickering.

Finally, Sylvia took the problem to her family doctor and then to her priest. What about the children, her pupils—could she hurt them in any way? Both men were certain that she couldn't; but at her insistence, they referred her to a psychiatrist. This physician interviewed Sylvia extensively and subjected her to a series of tests. At last he responded, "I see a young woman who has a great devotion to her family and who wants very much to please. Is that bad? Hardly, as long as she remembers to please herself as well."

Sylvia breathed a sigh of both exasperation and relief when he concluded, "You're quite normal, but something paranormal is going on." She knew *that*.

Again, Francine was of no help, refusing to even discuss the question of Sylvia's sanity. "Of course, you must teach. It will be an important part of your training," was all that she could or would say. Often, when Sylvia brought up the question of her sanity, Francine would disappear as if annoyed.

Finally, with considerable trepidation, Sylvia arranged for an interview with Sister Regina Mary, the principal of a small parochial school. Within an hour she emerged with the promise of a contract. Sylvia would be the only lay teacher in a faculty otherwise comprised of nuns.

In September 1956, one month short of her twentieth birthday, she began her teaching career. It was the first job, teaching or otherwise, that she had ever held, and she was terrified. "Will they like me?" she asked Francine again while driving to school the first day.

"Of course they will," the spirit replied in her no-nonsense fashion. "Haven't you spent years preparing for this?"

The reminder was of little help. Sylvia had begun to fear that all her past efforts had been misdirected. She'd dressed carefully that morning, discarding several choices before selecting a tweed suit with a tight skirt and a loose-fitting Chanel jacket. Sylvia had grown to her full height of five feet, seven inches, and was slim enough to be a model if she'd desired. Following Ski's departure, she'd cut the long red hair he'd so admired as a ritual gesture of independence. Getting out of the car with her lecture easel and her empty briefcase, she nervously patted her ducktail hairdo into place. Inside the school, fifty-five students waited for her. The impact of their eyes was palpable as she entered the assigned classroom and carefully set up her easel, glad to have something to hide behind.

"I'm your teacher for the year," she announced, and then she turned and wrote her name on the board in big, bold letters. "Sylvia Shoemaker." A boy in the front row snickered. Sylvia turned. "Now then, what are you laughing at?"

"Nothing."

"I'd really like to know," she persisted.

He laughed again, looking around at his friends for support. "I just wondered if your father made shoes."

Sylvia took a breath, then asked, "What's your name?"

"Ronald Necessary."

She suppressed a sigh of relief, thinking that God must

certainly be with her on this one. "No, Ronald, my father doesn't make shoes," she answered, "but we'll see before the year's out just how necessary you are to this class." The other children roared. Score one for Shoemaker and zero for the class bully.

In addition to her traditional teaching efforts, Sylvia sometimes held the wastebasket for the children when they threw up and occasionally she pulled their teeth. She showed them how to close their eyes and visualize what they wanted to be. And every day she told them how much she loved them.

None of the children ever seemed to think it strange that their teacher knew that they were angry or upset because they hadn't had any breakfast or had witnessed a violent argument at home or overheard an older sister tearfully announce that she was pregnant. No one ever said, "How do you know?" when the teacher took them aside for a reassuring little chat. It was simply taken for granted that Miss Shoemaker knew everything.

Late on a Friday afternoon in November, Sylvia sat at her desk grading papers. With a happy sigh she set the last one aside and sat back surveying the room. The basement classroom might be the least desirable one in the school, but it was *her* room and she loved it. Besides, she'd made it all so bright and cheerful with pumpkins and autumn leaves that you hardly noticed that there weren't any windows. Sylvia's confidence was growing. Some of the spit-and-polish shine was off the patent-leather teacher, but the enthusiasm had endured. "What do you think, Grandma?" she asked aloud. There was no answer, but Sylvia felt a warm glow envelop her. Happily, she gathered up her belongings and carefully locked the door behind her. That evening she and her friend, Maggie, treated themselves to dinner and a movie.

The next afternoon the phone rang. It was Sister Regina Mary. Sylvia caught her breath fearfully. The school principal never called on weekends. She must have done something awful, but what?

"Is everything all right?" she forced herself to ask.

"Well, yes and no," the nun answered.

It's my teaching, Sylvia thought, her old fears returning. A few weeks of student teaching simply hadn't prepared her for the responsibility of a whole class of her own. How could she have imagined that everything was going smoothly?

"Tell me what it is," she was almost whispering.

"I don't know how to begin—"

"Please, Sister," Sylvia urged.

"I hope you won't think I'm crazy," said Sister Regina Mary apologetically, "but the strangest thing happened just now."

"Won't you tell me, Sister?"

Haltingly, the woman began to explain. "I came to the school this afternoon to finish some reports. Naturally, the school was deserted. I was in my office working when I heard a noise downstairs. I knew I was the only one there and I couldn't imagine who could have gotten in without setting off the alarm."

Relieved, Sylvia could't help smiling as she thought of the school, a veritable fortress. The nun continued, "The more I listened, the more it sounded like someone walking, so I picked up my crucifix and ventured down to the lower level."

Sylvia smiled again. "Lower level" was a euphemism if there ever was one for a basement complete with furnace and ducts. "The door was open, which in itself was strange because all the teachers are expected to lock their rooms before leaving."

"Oh, I did, I did, I remember locking it," Sylvia interrupted.

"Yes, I know you did," Sister Regina Mary agreed. "I always check everything myself before I leave. Your room was properly locked last night, but just a few minutes ago I looked in and the door was wide open and there in the middle of the room was an elderly lady."

"What was she doing?" Sylvia asked, mystified.

"Nothing, just looking around. I asked if I could help her and she said, 'No, just tell Sylvia I wanted her to know I think she's doing fine. I just stopped by to have a look at her room.' "

"Did you ask her name?" Sylvia spoke very softly.

"Yes, but all she said was, 'Never mind, she'll know.' I went back upstairs to answer the phone. When I returned, she was gone. There's just no way that she could have gotten in or out without my seeing her or without triggering the alarm. I don't mind telling you, Sylvia, I just don't know what to make of it."

"What did she look like?" Sylvia inquired, beginning to tremble.

"She was about five feet, seven inches, with pure white hair done in a kind of Gibson Girl style. She wore a navy blue dress and smelled of lavender. The scent lingered in the room after she left. Do you know her?"

"Yes."

"What's the meaning of it, Sylvia? Who was it?" The principal's voice was suddenly stern.

"My grandmother."

"But how did she get in and out?"

"It was easy for her."

"What do you mean?"

"She's dead."

"I see." The nun abruptly changed the subject to a trivial school matter and soon terminated the conversation. The incident was never discussed again.

Grandma Ada's visit was a turning point in Sylvia's professional life. It was affirmation that she was, indeed, at the right place at the right time doing the right thing. She would never doubt her sanity again.

CHAPTER FOUR

Growing Pains

SYLVIA laughed so hard, she cried. She cried so hard, she laughed. Determined to forget Ski, she threw her energies into teaching, into parties, into readings. It didn't help. It wasn't enough. Nothing was enough.

Then one day a nun, one of her teaching colleagues, asked Sylvia for a reading. That was nothing new. Sylvia had inadvertently revealed her gift in high school when, psychically aware that a teacher was grieving over her family's financial loss, she'd come forward to offer reassurance. Word had quickly spread among the sisters until eventually they all had come to her.

But this request was different. The nun who tentatively approached was in her mid fifties. "Could you tell me what my life might have been like if I hadn't become a nun?" she asked. "There was a man. I loved him very much, but . . ."

In her mind's eye, Sylvia got a clear picture of a vital, handsome man in his early twenties. "He loved you, too, but there was so much pressure from your family. You just weren't able to stand up to them."

The nun nodded. "Yes, that's right. At the time, I felt there was nothing else that I could do, but now, sometimes I think of him and wonder . . ."

Sylvia hugged her spontaneously. "Of course you do, but I'm afraid I can't tell you anything about what your life might have been. What I read are blueprints. Yours

57

was to be a nun and you're following that blueprint. There's nothing else to read. The life you're leading is the one you were always meant to lead."

After the sister had left, Sylvia sat for a long time speculating about her own blueprint. For a short time, Ski had been her entire life. She loved him now as much as ever, but had accepted the fact that he could never be hers. Sylvia mourned her lover as though he were dead for, indeed, he was dead to her. She adored teaching and now took pride in knowing that she was good at it, but that wasn't enough. No matter how much of herself Sylvia poured into her career, it was never enough. An enormous void remained. Her life lacked purpose.

That evening Sylvia called her priest, Father O'Cannon, and made an appointment. The two talked for hours. "Perhaps the reason that you knew Ski's love and yet were strong enough to deny it is that you were meant to be a nun," he suggested.

Sylvia, remembering her childhood fascination with convent life, listened thoughtfully. Throughout her growing-up years, the church had been a refuge, providing solace and retreat from the ongoing chaos at home. A few weeks later, without discussing her plans with anyone, Sylvia sat down with Father O'Cannon and petitioned to enter the Franciscan order.

The formalities would take six months, she was told. Sylvia continued her life without change. "It's the only way you can be truly certain that convent life is for you," Father O'Cannon assured her. Since Ski's departure, Sylvia had dated a number of young men and finally one special one, John Elwood.

John was a big, gentle teddy bear type whose self-appointed mission was to heal Sylvia's broken heart. One evening, as they sat drinking tea, he broached the subject of Ski. "I know about it," he said. "I've made a point of finding out about you."

"Why?" she asked, her great brown eyes searching his face.

"Because I care," he replied, meeting her gaze. It was she who looked away.

"It doesn't matter, honey. I'm here to help you get over it," John assured her. In the background, a record played; Billie Holiday was singing, "And maybe some day a baby will climb upon your knee . . ." His hands reached for her, pulled her toward him.

They sat for what seemed like hours. She felt soothed and comforted, very much like a baby. It was wonderful. Finally John broke the silence. "The only thing is, I don't know if I'm ready for this trance thing you do."

"Oh, hell," she said, and she started to pull away, remembering Joe Behm. Sylvia liked doing readings and wasn't about to give them up again.

"I don't mind the psychic stuff. It's that Francine. I just don't think I like the idea of you leaving your body and some other gal taking over and talking through you. How will I know who's who?"

Relieved, Sylvia giggled. "You'd know, all right. Francine's very different from me, very independent. Men aren't all that important to her."

"Ah, one of those lesbians. A lesbian spirit, that's intriguing."

"No, it's more like she's beyond all of it. There's a male entity in her life, but she's very much her own person— if you can say that about a spirit."

"But I still don't like the idea of her just coming in and taking over."

"That's only happened once," Sylvia explained. "The psychology department of the University of Kansas City was offering a special hypnosis class. I signed up out of curiosity. During a demonstration, I slipped into a trance and Francine took over. It was her way of showing me what trancing was all about. It's never happened again.

The last thing she wants is to dominate me and she would never, never play tricks on anyone."

John's fears were allayed and the two settled into a pleasant, easy relationship. Some of the pain connected with Ski had subsided to a dull ache that could sometimes be forgotten. Sylvia loved teaching and in a few months would become a nun. In the meantime, John was a pleasant companion. Despite his easy manner, Sylvia's new friend was sophisticated and intellectual. She found him quite different from Ski or the Rockhurst boys she'd been dating for years, and that added to his charm. A Princeton graduate, John was finishing out his Army time shuffling papers. He came from a wealthy family and envisioned a dazzling future that didn't include Kansas City.

Their romance had a bittersweet "ships passing in the night" quality to it that appealed to Sylvia. They laughed a lot and flirted, Sylvia refusing to take any of it seriously. She was surprised, then, by John's obvious sadness when his military service ended and he prepared to return to his home in Peru, Indiana. "You will write to me, won't you?" he urged her. "You won't do anything foolish like commit yourself to anyone else? You will let me come and visit you at Thanksgiving?"

"Yes. No. Yes," she answered, still laughing, but a little puzzled by his unexpected ardor.

John left and Sylvia found herself missing him, much more than she'd anticipated. She looked forward to his letters and answered them by return mail. Sometimes she found herself speculating about the kind of life they might have together. A man who loved her, children of her own—they were surely valid considerations that deserved to be weighed against the advantages of convent life. More than anything, Sylvia wanted to be settled and secure. Marriage or a convent? The painful uncertainty again emerged; the need to decide once and for all loomed large as her twenty-first birthday approached.

Weeks before, Sylvia had picked up psychically that her parents were planning a surprise party for her. She purposefully avoided making plans for that Friday night, but when the evening arrived and she came home from school, the house was quiet. Finally, unable to bear the suspense, she asked Celeste, "What happened to my party?"

Her mother gasped, half annoyed, half marveling, as she had so many times over the years. "Can't we keep anything from you? We had to postpone it until tomorrow night."

At loose ends, she called her friend, Maggie. "What shall we do tonight?"

"I have a date," Maggie told her. "Jerry finally asked me out."

"Jerry, the policeman? The one you've been after for months?"

"The very one. Suppose I call him and see if he's got a friend?"

"A blind date? I don't think so. I'm sort of going with John and besides, I'm almost a nun."

They both laughed, realizing how outrageous it sounded. "I'd really like you to come," Maggie persisted. "I'm awfully nervous. Having you there would really help. We'll stay together and even if you don't like him, we can have fun just going out. You don't want to stay home on your birthday, do you?"

Sylvia didn't, and Maggie called back a few minutes later and announced that Jerry did indeed have a friend. The two officers were to get off duty at nine; Sylvia, still feeling apprehensive, went with Maggie to meet them at the police station.

Gary Dufresne had sharp features redeemed in Sylvia's opinion by intense blue eyes. Not bad really, for a blind date, she decided. "I'm Sylvia Shoemaker," she introduced herself, adding, when he remained silent, "I'm a schoolteacher."

Maggie had forgotten all about introductions; she'd also forgotten her promise that they'd remain together. "Jerry and I will go in his car and you can meet us somewhere," she announced.

Gary smiled at last, a rather nice smile, Sylvia thought. He took her arm as they walked to his own car. She sat far over to the right, suddenly recalling her father's repeated admonitions that cops were "no good." They could rape you and no one could do a thing about it. As if able to read her thoughts, Gary turned into a dark alley and parked.

Sylvia tensed, her hand grasping the door handle, but Gary merely got out of the car and came around to open the door for her. Together they walked down the alley and into the back of what turned out to be a bar, Sylvia's first.

What a relief to find Maggie and Jerry already seated in a booth. There was a flurry of small talk and then a lull, broken by Gary. "Now Miss Sylvia Shoemaker, schoolteacher, if we were alone, I'd ask you to tell me about yourself."

Sylvia hesitated, but not Maggie, who explained, "She's part Jewish and Catholic and she can tell people about their future."

"A fortune-teller, huh?" Gary remarked. He eyed Sylvia speculatively, then added, "I've never cared much for Catholics, or Jews either."

Sylvia instantly dismissed theirs as an amazingly brief, uncomplicated association and looked about the room. It was cheap and shabby. She felt a wave of misery and loneliness. Sylvia was picking up vibes again and they were awful. The next incident did nothing to relieve her depression.

There was a commotion in the back of the room. Gary leaped to his feet and ran toward the noise. Someone had fallen out of a phone booth. As Gary approached, the man grabbed at his legs. Instantly Gary drew his gun and pointed it menacingly. "Get up and get out of here," he ordered. Without hesitation, the man rose and fled from the bar.

"Do you always carry a gun—even when you're off duty?" Sylvia asked.

"Always."

"Why did you pull it just now?"

"To scare him." Gary's impatient tone indicated he wanted no more discussion. Sylvia was glad a few moments later when he suggested they leave. The two couples separated, Sylvia and Gary returning to the car in silence. "Where to?" he asked.

"Take me back to the station, my car's parked close by."

"You haven't been around much, have you?"

"No, I don't suppose I have."

Neither of them said anything more until he unlocked her car for her. "How about going out some night?"

"Sure," Sylvia replied, though she had no intention of seeing him again. She was surprised by his suggestion; it seemed so obvious that she wasn't his type. She wanted nothing more than to end the evening as quickly as possible. Explanations or arguments would only have prolonged it.

"Maybe that's the way cops are—unpredictable," Maggie suggested the next day, adding, "What do you think of Jerry?"

"It doesn't matter," Sylvia replied. "He's not the one for you."

"Now you're beginning to sound like my mother."

Sylvia shrugged. "Sorry about that," she said. "I have to tell you what I see. Jerry's fine, but he'll only be a short-term thing in your life. There's someone else—you haven't met him yet." She went on to describe the heavy-set red-haired man her friend would eventually marry. "He's in the Army. You'll meet him in a year; six months later you'll be married."

"And what about you?" Maggie challenged.

"If only I knew. The longer I teach, the more I'm around children, the more I'd like to have my own. But then I think about the church, the peace, the wonderful tranquility that it offers. Who can tell about marriage? Suppose I ended up like my mother."

"I should think Francine could give you some help with this."

"She's no help at all. The best I can get from her is that my blueprint already exists and I have only to follow it. What good is a message like that?"

While Sylvia puzzled over her future, John's letters arrived regularly. There were frequent phone calls, too. Sylvia found his deep voice very reassuring, as comforting, she reflected, as Gregorian chants.

October drew to a close. It was Halloween night and Sylvia was ready for some excitement. When the phone rang, it was Gary, inviting her out for a late dinner.

"Why not?" she surprised herself by responding, but she had barely hung up when her misgivings began. A few minutes later she called him back. "I'm awfully sorry, but my aunt's visiting us and she just broke her leg. I have to drive her to the hospital."

"That's a shame," he said. "I was really looking forward to seeing you."

"I *am* sorry," Sylvia said, "maybe another time." But she vowed there'd never be one. That evening, she and Maggie went to a horror movie. "Gary called a few minutes after you left," Maggie's mother informed them when they returned. "I had no idea you'd lied to him, Sylvia. Naturally, when he asked where you girls were, I told him. Really, I should think you'd know better than to tell such a ridiculous story to a policeman."

"I never lie to anybody, I hate lies. It was stupid of me and I'll never do it again," Sylvia said and meant it.

The incident wasn't the end of Gary. To her surprise, he called again and again. The fourth time she gave in; but insisted that Maggie accompany them on a date. Gary's mild disgust was thinly veiled and this time Sylvia was certain she'd seen the last of him.

The night before Thanksgiving, John arrived. He talked with Sylvia about her future in the church—she saw no reason to mention Gary. John was having enough trouble thinking of her as a nun.

Sylvia listened with interest as John told her about his return to civilian life. "Mother persuaded me to spend the winter with her. I've been away so long and with Father gone, she gets lonely," John explained. In the late spring he'd be moving to Chicago to begin his career as an executive in the family insurance company.

"Chicago's a very exciting place; they've even written a song about it," he reminded her before leaving the following Sunday. Sylvia promised she'd spend Christmas with him and his family in Indiana.

When the young police officer took to dropping by unexpectedly after work, Sylvia realized that Gary wasn't the type to be easily discouraged. Though exasperated at first, she began to look forward to his visits when she discovered that beneath the laconic exterior was not only a dry sense of humor but an agile mind. Gary and his friends were older, more worldly than the men she'd known. Their cops-and-robbers world was new and exciting to her. When two whole weeks passed with only fleeting thoughts of Ski, Sylvia began to hope she was getting over him.

As the days flew by, Christmas was approaching, and with it her promised trip to Indiana. Sylvia, traveling alone for the first time, felt a glow of anticipation as she boarded the train. It was still the era of polished wood club cars and porters in white starched uniforms. Despite some trepidation about John's family, she felt very sophisticated in her new suit. In one of the few significant intuitive insights that Sylvia had ever had about herself, she received a clear picture of a protective mother and two doting sisters.

The train pulled into Peru, Indiana, at twilight. The town, blanketed in newly fallen snow, looked like a fairy tale village. John was waiting, ruddy, smiling, big, and warm. "Come on, Mom has dinner waiting," he said after a giant bear hug. It sounded cheery enough.

They drove out into the suburbs. "That's Cole Porter's house," John said, pointing to a mansion, "and this is my house." He drove through the iron gateway that flanked the drive of the equally impressive estate next door. As they approached, Sylvia stared in amazement at the magnificent facade before her. "Why, it looks like Dragonwyck!" she exclaimed, remembering a Gothic movie she'd seen as a child.

The house, with its turrets, its towers, and its broad, sloping grounds, was a monument to old money. Sylvia tried not to feel intimidated, but she was. The greeting extended by John's mother merely added to her growing discomfort. "Miss Shoemaker, how pleasant of you to grace us with your presence," Mrs. Elwood said, standing back to inspect her.

Sylvia struggled to think of an appropriately effusive reply, but couldn't. "Thank you," she murmured, extending her hand as if across an icy chasm to Mrs. Elwood. John's mother was a short, stout woman with rigidly styled hair and a thin, pursed mouth. There was an air of disdain about her features as though she'd either tasted or smelled something unpleasant.

John's sisters turned out to be clones of their mother. The holiday stretched out before Sylvia like a life sentence.

"Are you having fun?" John asked the next day. "Aren't they wonderful?" He was shocked when Sylvia suggested that his family didn't like her. "They love you as much as I do," he insisted, and he appeared to honestly believe it.

After four days of confinement, Sylvia insisted that John take her out alone. He reluctantly agreed, but his resolve weakened at his mother's stricken face.

"That's all right," Mrs. Elwood said, her hand straying to her heart. "Just go along. I'll be fine."

"Is anything wrong?" John asked, bending anxiously over the great wing chair where she sat.

"Nothing really, just my heart. Now and then it acts up a bit—nothing for you two young people to worry about. I'll be happy here all alone, knowing that you're having a good time."

"We'd better not go," John said.

Sylvia could stand it no longer. "Whatever you decide to do, I'm going for a walk." She was already out the great, massive door when John caught up with her. The light of the full moon was bright on the snow. It was a night out of a Russian fairy tale, but the couple scarcely noticed. The snow crunched noisily under their feet, the only sound, for neither of them could find words to express their disappointment. Finally, John began a halting discourse on his career plans. Sylvia had heard it all before but now doubted that he would ever leave home. She responded absently, knowing John's mind was really on his mother's heart, an organ that Sylvia suspected would outlast her own.

Sylvia wasn't able to bring their conversation around to the situation; perhaps she didn't really try. Finally they trudged back through the snow to the house. Pausing just inside the door, John kissed her goodnight. He was staying with his married sister because Mrs. Elwood didn't think it proper that he sleep under the same roof with an unmarried woman.

Sylvia hurried up to her room, hoping to avoid Mrs. Elwood. As she was preparing for bed, she received a precognitive vision. John's mother was planning a surprise party, during which Sylvia's engagement to John would be announced. Sylvia had never felt less centered, more insecure. Without any further thought, she made her way to the upstairs phone. Her hands were trembling as she dialed. It was her father who answered.

"How do you feel about it?" he asked after she'd told him the story.

"If I ever had any idea of marrying John, it's gone now. I'd be marrying his mother right along with him and probably his snooty sisters, too."

"Then there's nothing keeping you there. The sooner you leave, the better. You've got your return ticket." Typically protective, he offered, "I'll call the depot in the morning and get a train schedule for you."

"Thank you, Daddy."

"For what?"

"Just for being there." She was trying not to cry.

A little choked up himself, he changed the subject. "Speaking of people being there, Gary has been over here every night since you left."

"How come?"

"Come on, Sylvia, you can figure that one out. The guy's crazy about you."

"Don't tell me that! I've enough to worry about right here. I want out!"

"I'll get on it," he promised.

Just as Sylvia was hanging up the phone, she heard a clicking sound. She was certain Mrs. Elwood had been listening. Sylvia hurried back to her room with the very unpleasant sense that she was being spied upon. Finally, after lying awake for hours, she fell into a fitful sleep. It was late morning when she awakened. Dressing quickly, Sylvia hurried downstairs to find John and his mother waiting for her in the breakfast room. One look at their faces verified her suspicions; they were clearly aware of her feelings. "I want to leave today," she informed them.

John banged his cup down in frustration, but before he could say a word, Mrs. Elwood spoke. "I hope you're not getting angry at your mother, Johnnie. It isn't I who disappointed you."

That was enough for Sylvia; she turned away intending to go back to her room and John rose to his feet and crossed the room in an instant, pulling her to him. "I love you," he said in a hoarse, pleading voice. His mother's hand went to her heart.

"Not enough—or *not as much*, I'm afraid," Sylvia said, thinking of Mrs. Elwood. Pulling free, she went to the hall phone, and, without a word, dialed her home number. Once again, her father answered. "How soon can I get a train out of here?" she asked.

"There's one at six forty-five this evening. It'll get you in around midnight. We'll be there to meet you."

"I'll be on it."

"Oh, no you won't! You're not going anywhere," Mrs. Elwood, now standing beside her, said with quiet authority.

Sylvia gasped, "What do you mean?"

"Exactly what I said. You're not going to embarrass John or myself. A gathering has been planned. All our friends have been invited. I expect you to be there."

"I heard that!" Sylvia's father was yelling into the phone. "Tell her if you're not on that train, I'll rent a helicopter and land on her damned house."

Sylvia didn't have to repeat the message, for Mrs. Elwood could hear every word. Her face turned white. "Johnnie is well rid of you," she said and walked stiffly away.

"Be there, Daddy, I'm coming home." Sylvia hung up the phone and hurried up the broad staircase to her room.

She'd barely finished packing her few things when John knocked on the door. It had been his air of gentleness that had first appealed to her; now she reflected that the gentleness was possibly weakness.

"Why don't we go out somewhere for lunch?" he suggested.

Sylvia agreed, but insisted on taking her bag with her. She had no intention of ever returning to the Ellwoods' house. They drove through the snowy countryside for hours before John finally took her to the station. Lunch had been a desultory affair. John wanted nothing more than to change her mind, but there was nothing left to say. Sylvia didn't need psychic ability to predict what life would be like with Mrs. Elwood for a mother-in-law. Beyond that, the image of John as he catered to his mother was an even more potent warning. Sylvia was relieved to see the train waiting and was eager to board.

John got on with her and together they walked through car after car filled with holiday passengers. At last, they found a vacant seat by a window. John placed her bag on the shelf above her and then sat down, holding both Sylvia's hands in his. "Was it the party? Maybe you just felt that you were being rushed," he suggested.

She shook her head sadly, but he ignored the gesture. "We talked so often about the kind of life we could have. You know I love you. I really thought you loved me, too."

Sylvia's eyes filled with tears. "I do—in a way. But it just wasn't meant to be." The train jolted, then very slowly began to move. "I'll never forget you, John," she promised. "You were there for me when I really needed it. I'll always remember what a good friend you were."

Reluctantly, John rose and she with him. They hugged briefly and then he hurried from the moving car. Watching from the window, she saw him leap onto the platform. The train was moving faster now. John was gone.

Sylvia stopped waving and leaned back against the

leather cushions. She listened to the click of the rails, a very comforting sound. Ski had said goodbye to her, she had said goodbye to John. Another chapter was ended. Outside, the snow fell heavily against the darkening sky, but the interior of the car felt warm and safe. The pressures of the previous months faded away. A sense of peace and confidence enveloped Sylvia. She was going home. This was a moment frozen in time, complete, and to be remembered always.

CHAPTER FIVE

Following the Blueprint

SYLVIA'S train had been delayed by near-blizzard conditions. At half-past three in the morning, when it finally pulled into Kansas City, the station was filled. Revelers celebrating the new year were everywhere. Scanning the many faces, Sylvia saw her father almost immediately, then Celeste, and behind her, Gary.

"When your dad said you were coming home, I thought I'd better meet your train," he explained. "I've got this party—I'd like you to go with me. If I waited till tomorrow to ask you, you'd probably have something else to do—like taking your aunt to the hospital or something."

Sylvia winced. Her father answered before she could open her mouth. "Of course she'll go."

"Will you, Sylvia?" Gary persisted.

"Why not?" She was too tired to respond to the embarrassing jibe.

By the time they reached the house, Sylvia had nodded off. It was Gary who awakened her. "You really will come? You won't forget or change your mind again?" he gently prodded while helping her out of the car.

Sylvia agreed dazedly, her thoughts only of sleep. It had been a very long day. "I promise," she said. At the front door, Gary kissed her quickly and was off into the icy dawn.

That evening, after sleeping most of the day, Sylvia felt refreshed and almost happy. She dressed with special care, accenting a sleekly simple black silk dress with a pearl necklace and earrings—her father's Christmas gift. Her hair, allowed to grow again, was swept into a French twist. At twenty-one, she'd loved and lost. Hardly a woman of the world, Sylvia still sought to pass for one. She winked at herself in the mirror, suddenly pleased with the image reflected there.

The young man who greeted her downstairs shared more of her newfound confidence. It was a Gary she'd never seen before. He actually appeared nervous. Their arrival at the party was greeted with eager enthusiasm. The police officers and their wives who crowded about them seemed oddly conspiratorial. Sylvia began to feel like the key character in a mystery plot.

A pretty, dark-haired young woman approached and introduced herself. "I'm Barbara Crowther. Don works with Gary." Sylvia liked her instantly and before long the two were chatting like old friends.

"I'm so glad Gary met you," Barbara confided. "He used to keep Don out half the night. Now I finally get to see a little of my husband. Besides, I can tell you're good for Gary."

"We're not really going together," Sylvia hastened to explain. "We're simply good friends."

Just then, Gary appeared, "May I borrow Sylvia for a minute? I've got a big deal to discuss."

"Of course," Barbara agreed, smiling. "I've a notion that she and I are going to be seeing a lot of one another from now on."

Puzzling over Barbara's knowing manner, Sylvia followed Gary into the strangely deserted family room.

"Did your folks say anything?" he asked as they seated themselves on the large couch.

"About what?"

"Never mind."

"What is this?"

"Don't you know—psychically, I mean?"

"Really, Gary, if I've told you once, I've told you a thousand times, I don't 'know' everything! Maybe once in a while a message comes through for me, but not often and never when I try."

"It may seem a little strange to you at first—since we haven't exactly been dating—but I've known since the first time I saw you."

"Known what?" Sylvia asked, feeling herself drawing away.

"I'll get to that in a minute. Maybe I should tell you a little about myself. I never like to talk about personal stuff, but now I guess I'd better. I was an Army brat. I lived in nearly every state in the union, then went to high school in Japan and spent four years in the Marines. I've been with the police department for nearly three years. I like it here. I'm ready to settle down. I *want* to settle down." In Gary's mind, everything was about to be settled.

"That's all very interesting," Sylvia prompted him, "but I've been through a lot lately. I want to know where this conversation's going."

"I'm getting to that." He turned to face her squarely. "I've loved you since the first time I saw you two years ago."

"Two years ago!" Sylvia exclaimed, gigging nervously. "We just met two months ago."

Gary smiled. "Some psychic you are! You don't even know what's going on in *this* world. Do you remember two years ago when your friend, Maggie, had a stalled car on the college campus? A police officer came to take the report. Do you recall him?"

Sylvia remembered the incident very well. The principal's voice announcing through the loudspeaker that Mary Marguerite Ryan was to report to her car. Maggie had been doubled over with menstrual cramps at the time.

"You go, Sylvia," she'd pleaded. "They probably want to tow my car somewhere. You take care of it."

Sylvia arrived in time to see a policeman writing a ticket. He explained to her that he'd been called in to investigate the possibility that the car was stolen. "Either the young lady has to have the car fixed or she can expect to have it towed at her own expense," he'd explained.

Sylvia had been furious. "Don't you cops have anything better to do than harass college girls? Why aren't you out catching criminals?" she'd demanded to know.

"Some temper you got, cutie," he'd commented, not in the least annoyed.

"Don't you cutie me!" she'd snapped.

"What's your name?"

"Sylvia Shoemaker. Are you going to give me a ticket, too?"

"Not this time," he'd said, handing her Maggie's ticket, which actually turned out to be merely a warning. "I can still remember you flouncing out of that office. 'I certainly hope you fill your quota of tickets,' " he mimicked.

"That was you?" Sylvia asked incredulously.

Gary nodded. "I was determined to find you, but there must be a hundred Shoemakers in Kansas City—and they all spell the name differently. Finally I gave up calling, but never hoping. You can't imagine how I felt when I saw you that night in the station. It was like a dream had come true for me."

"But why didn't you say something?"

"I kept thinking that you'd remember me at some point, but instead you kept doing everything you could think of to get rid of me."

The story seemed terribly romantic to Sylvia, suddenly very much aware of how badly she'd treated Gary. She studied him. He reminded her of a big cat—not an unattractive image.

"I found out right away about that guy in Indiana—I gather that's over now," Gary continued, taking her hands in one of his. "I also know you've petitioned to become a nun. I hope you won't go through with it because you'd be ruining all my plans."

"What plans?" Sylvia asked, her voice almost a whisper.

"I found you again in 1958. I want to marry you in 1959." Before Sylvia could say a word, he'd reached into his pocket and brought out a blue velvet box. When she didn't take it, Gary removed the top to reveal the largest diamond she'd ever seen.

The events of the last twenty-four hours were just too much. Sylvia began to cry. Gary put his arms around her reassuringly. "You'll get used to the idea, honey. Your parents are already delighted. They like me. You know they weren't very happy about either of your plans. Moving to Chicago was bad enough—but the convent! They're praying you won't enter. Either way, they'd be losing you. You're everything to them, you know that."

She did indeed know. The choice between John and the convent had been only part of her dilemma. From the beginning, there'd been a missing piece of the puzzle, a piece that she'd attempted to ignore. Sylvia had always been the glue that held the Shoemaker family together. What would happen to them without her?

Sylvia imagined her mother's loneliness if she were to finally lose Bill after all these years. And then her father— I am the light in his eyes, she acknowledged matter-of-factly. He had always seen her as the best, the prettiest, the cleverest person in the world. Knowing it, she'd excelled. At first it had been school; Sylvia learned so fast she'd skipped a grade. Later she'd become her father's little sweetheart. As a girl, she'd been barely into her teens before they'd begun entering dance contests together and winning. Sylvia remembered the black lace dress he'd bought her when she was sixteen. It had cost a hundred dollars, a fortune in those days. How proud he'd been of her when she stepped forward to receive the first-prize trophy they'd won together.

But now—didn't she deserve her own life, a life apart from the needs and desires of others? Sylvia shook her head as though to clear it and returned to Gary. "I don't know what's best for them, me, anybody," she admitted.

He closed her hand over the ring. "Keep it awhile and think about it. Please, Sylvia, it won't hurt to just think about it."

At that moment, the other guests burst excitedly into the room. It was obvious that they could contain their impatience no longer.

"Congratulations!"

"How thrilling!"

"We're so happy for you both!"

"When's the wedding?"

Once again, Sylvia felt she was the central character in a drama, one that was becoming more romantic and exciting all the time. It was hard not to get caught up in it all. "We'll see," she murmured. "We'll see."

Returning home in the early hours of 1959, she found her parents waiting up anxiously. It was obvious that they were solidly behind Gary. Their reasoning was persuasive. After all his years of traveling, Gary was eager to set down roots—happily in Kansas City. Sylvia's life with him could be really good, giving her the children she wanted, and the security she needed. And her parents supported a match which would bring them the grandchildren they longed for and keep their little girl from straying far away. Why, there was even a nice apartment for rent just down the street. Celeste was certain that it was just the thing for her daughter. She and Bill would be more than happy to help with the furnishings.

Sylvia listened absently. Perhaps they were right. She admired Gary's self-assurance. No doubt about it, here was a man who knew what he wanted and went right for it. She could learn a lot from his single-mindedness.

When John Elwood called later that day, Sylvia told him about the proposal. "But what about us, Sylvia?" was his response, an even weaker one than she'd anticipated.

It was a bitter young woman who still longed for a lost sweetheart who answered. "Gary wants to marry me in April," she said. "If you can detach yourself from your mother and marry me before then, okay. Otherwise, I'm going ahead with it." Once said, the words even shocked Sylvia. She'd spoken spontaneously, without thinking, aware only that she'd lost Ski and that John had rejected her in favor of his mother. Now it was she who was calling the shots. Without realizing it, Sylvia had made a major life decision as easily, as heedlessly, as one might change TV channels.

John made it even easier for her when he announced, "Mother needs me for some family business, she really does, and I can't possibly be free until August."

"Fine. That settles it," she told him. "I'm getting married on April second."

"What do you know about this guy?" asked John, attempting to reason with her.

"I know that he loves me and I know he's a man who lets nothing stand in his way. That's enough for me."

The next day Sylvia went to see Father O'Cannon. Telling him of her plans was more difficult, but there was some compensation in the marvelous sense of relief that accompanies the final resolution of a difficult issue. The assurance it brought carried her through the interview. At last it was settled once and for all. Sylvia would have children of her own, she was marrying a strong, dynamic man who excited her. She would soon have her own home. And in pursuing this course, she was pleasing her parents and possibly even preserving their marriage. Happier and more relaxed than she's been in months, Sylvia felt almost giddy.

Soon her life centered entirely around Gary. For the next few weeks she taught, came home, rested. At midnight, Gary got off duty and they spent three hours together. Then Sylvia went to bed and slept—if she was lucky—until it was time to get up and teach again.

Friends called, leaving messages, but there wasn't much time to return their calls. Finally, one Sunday afternoon a group dropped by. When they pressed Sylvia about her absence, she flashed her diamond mischievously and replied. "I've been busy."

There were excited shrieks. "You and John finally did it! When's the wedding?"

"April second, but not John," she announced, enjoying their surprise and suspense. She'd been part of this ingrown group for so long, the sudden transformation to mystery woman was delicious. She was heady with the knowledge of what she'd done on her own, without discussing it with anyone.

"Who is it?" they asked at once.

"Gary."

"Gary who?"

"You haven't met him yet. He's a policeman." Her elation began to dissipate in their silence—a silence, she realized, that implied doubt and concern. "He loves me," she added defensively.

"You can't know him very well."

"Two months—that's long enough," she insisted.

"And Francine, what does she say?" a friend who'd known Sylvia since grammar school asked.

"She says that I'm destined to follow my blueprint."

"What the hell does that mean?"

"Whatever it means, it's happening," Sylvia declared, briskly putting an end to their questions.

"Going all the way" before marriage was a mortal sin, but that didn't mean that it didn't happen. Sylvia wondered occasionally why Gary didn't even try. It must be because he respects me so much, she reasoned. Such reticence from a man who'd seen so much of life was touching. It also made life less complicated for her in the hectic weeks before the wedding.

Sylvia and Gary were married April 2, 1959, at St. James Church. The magnitude of what she was doing hit her finally the night before the ceremony. It was as though she'd awakened from a dream. "What am I doing?" she asked Maggie. "I don't love Gary. I don't even know him."

"It was a rebound romance; we all knew that," Maggie said. "We all tried to tell you."

Sylvia buried her face in her hands and began to cry softly.

"You don't have to go through with it," Maggie reminded her. "It's not too late to stop."

But for Sylvia it was. All the plans had been made—the invitations, the gowns, the flowers, the caterers, the music. For days, she'd been receiving wedding gifts. The priests, the attendants, her friends, her parents, and, of course, Gary, all were expecting her to fulfill her promise. How could she disappoint them?

The night was long, sleepless. Sylvia's mind raced, but she knew there was no acceptable alternative. The wedding would go on as planned. The next morning, Celeste greeted her with an elaborate breakfast, but all Sylvia could do was look at it. Such "jitters" were to be expected, her parents sagely agreed. The dishes were quickly cleared.

Celeste, Maggie, and Sharon helped Sylvia dress and then donned their own finery. Bill beamed at them proudly, certain that he would be escorting the best-looking women in Kansas City. Just as Sylvia was about to step into the car, a young man driving by slowed down and called out the window, "I just want to say that you're pretty as a picture." Sylvia's spirits lifted, but not for long.

In the crowded church, Sylvia was suffocating. She wanted to scream but no sound came from her smiling lips. Once again she performed on cue, walking down the aisle on her father's arm. As she knelt before the priest, she noticed that his shoes needed shining. Sylvia stole a look at Gary. Who was that stranger?

Then the final words—awful and irreversible—were spoken and the service was over. The newlyweds were walking back down the aisle and out the door amid a shower of rice. At the lavish reception, where champagne flowed freely, Sylvia discovered Gary in the adjoining bar drinking something stronger. Did he too have regrets, Sylvia wondered.

The time came for them to leave. Tears, hugs, goodbyes over, they were finally alone in Gary's car. For more than an hour they drove, halfhearted attempts at conversation going nowhere.

It was late Thursday afternoon. Both had to be back at work on Monday morning. "Where are we going?" Sylvia asked at last.

They were approaching a sign that read, Sedalia, Missouri. "This looks like as good a place as any," Gary said, turning into a Motor Inn with an adjoining restaurant. Gary ordered liver and onions for dinner; Sylvia had the same. Wasn't it the companionable thing to do? Both seemingly at a loss for words, the dinner stretched on interminably.

At last the check came. Gary paid it and they rose and walked silently to their room. It was drab, cheerless, ordinary. Sylvia turned on the radio. The tune playing was a current hit, *Love Is a Many Splendored Thing*. She scarcely knew whether to laugh or cry.

The debacle of her honeymoon was a stunning blow to Sylvia's self-esteem; typically, she blamed herself. It was ten days before the marriage was consummated. Lacking experience, Sylvia speculated endlessly—if only I were worldlier, sexier, prettier. Reared in a tradition that deferred to men in every way, it never occurred to her to challenge Gary or even to question him. It was years before Sylvia learned the whole story of her husband's tragic childhood. Later, much later, he confided that his mother had run off with a snake medicine salesman when he was two and that seven years later he'd discovered the body of his grandmother hanging from a self-tied noose.

At the time of her marriage, Sylvia knew only that the man who'd been so desperate to make her his wife, to bask in the warmth of her enthusiasm and humor, now seemed intent upon changing her, determined to mold her into another person entirely.

She had entered the marriage seeking comfort and approval and in their place found only criticism. Very soon Sylvia realized that nothing that she could ever do would satisfy Gary. But that didn't stop her from trying.

On the surface, theirs was a successful marriage. They were both gregarious and enjoyed a lively social life. Their private disappointments remained private. Sometimes Sylvia found a grim humor in her situation, remembering that she'd once wanted to be a nun. Then on December 9, 1959, at half-past nine in the evening, she became pregnant. Sylvia thought the event something of a miracle, considering the infrequency of their sexual intimacy. She was certain that she knew the very instant that conception had taken place. "Yes, you are, indeed, pregnant," Francine confirmed, telling Sylvia that her child would be a boy and would one day stand six feet, five inches tall.

Gary was furious when he heard the news and refused to speak to Sylvia for a week. He resented the financial responsibility and the intrusion into his life. For once, Gary's opinions didn't matter. Sylvia was wildly happy, for this was the child she'd longed for, the treasured entity who, for a short time at least, would be hers alone.

When, on a day early the following August, Gary asked

Sylvia what she was planning to give him for his birthday, she laughed and said, "A son." Paul Jon Dufresne was born nearly a month early, arriving at 2:32 on the afternoon of August 19, 1960—his father's birthday.

By the first week of September, Sylvia was back in school, teaching. Her joyous expectations proved short-lived. A postpartum depression was the last thing that she would have expected, yet week after week she walked through her tasks enveloped by a soul-crushing malaise. To make matters more difficult, Paul was a colicky baby. Gary, already resentful, was enraged by his crying. Sylvia was up half of every night walking the floor with the baby, trying to soothe him. Finally exhausted and totally dispirited, she begged Gary to allow her to stay home with their child for one year. He would have none of it. "We need your salary," he insisted. "Don't even think of quitting." Obediently, Sylvia handed Gary her paycheck of 276 dollars a month. She had no idea how much her husband made.

"Why do I have to go through all this?" she asked Francine. "Unless you experience many things now, you'll be unable to help others later," was the answer. Sylvia laughed aloud. With her own life a perpetual twilight of depression, how could she possibly help anyone else? But Francine promised, "One day you will be a star." Sylvia would gladly have settled for a good night's sleep.

As bad as things were, they could—and did—get worse. When Paul was five months old he caught the staph infection that was raging throughout the city. Sylvia watched, panic-stricken, as her baby's temperature shot up to 105 degrees and remained there. She was on the phone hourly to the doctor. The hospitals were full. All Sylvia could do was try to keep Paul comfortable with cold water baths and lots of water. She held him all night long.

The next morning, Paul's temperature was even higher. Frantically, Sylvia called the doctor. Then called him again and again. "I promise I'll let you know the minute there's a place for him," he attempted to soothe her. "In the meantime, just keep giving him baths." She hung up and carried Paul into the small bedroom of their apartment. The child was delirious; his head rolled from side to side as though to escape pain.

Helplessly, Sylvia sank into a rocking chair. "Please, God, don't let him die," she pleaded aloud, and then added, "Grandma, help me. I know you lost your Paul, please don't let me lose mine."

Sylvia had no sooner said the words than she felt a wave of cool air. Paul opened his eyes, then cooed and blinked. He seemed to be looking at something beyond her right shoulder. "Grandma, it's you!" Sylvia cried out, and just as she said the words, a mass card that had been wedged for years in the mirror of her dressing table actually flew into the air and landed on the floor at her feet. It read, "Ada C. Coil; Died July 13, 1954."

Sylvia was weeping uncontrollably when the phone rang. It was the doctor. There was a bed for Paul and she was to bring him in immediately. Sylvia was there in fifteen minutes and then waited alone for hours, unwilling to bother anyone. "If the baby dies, it's your fault," Gary had warned. Unaccountably, he blamed her for Paul's illness.

But Paul didn't die. After twenty-six hours in isolation, he began to recover. After a week, he was allowed to come home and a marked change quickly followed. It wasn't long before he was sleeping through the night, and so was Sylvia. Slowly her intense depression began to lift.

When Gary suggested, none too delicately, that she make more of a financial contribution, Sylvia knew that life had returned to normal. Obedient as ever, she got a Christmas job selling candy, and during the following summer she sold trailers. Their bank account grew rapidly and when it reached a few hundred dollars Gary decided that a house of their own was a testament to their upwardly mobile state. A cluster of tract homes was under construction nearby. The couple walked through the models and selected the one that Gary preferred. The down payment was made and Gary importantly directed Sylvia in the paperwork. A month later, their house completed, the Dufresnes went down to inspect it for the first time.

"There's something wrong here," Sylvia said as they stepped inside.

"What do you mean?" Gary asked, thumping the wall. "It looks okay to me."

"No, it's not okay, not at all. Something's wrong here. We don't belong here," Sylvia said, almost frantic.

"We'll belong as long as we manage the 104 dollars a month."

"I'm serious," she insisted, "we don't belong here."

"Don't give me that spook stuff. We paid for this place and we're moving in."

"The time has not yet come for you to be believed," Francine explained.

They moved in, but from the beginning things were wrong. Sylvia had selected a room on the top floor of the tri-level for Paul. It was the lightest and brightest in the house and had a sunny morning exposure. She'd taken great pleasure in planning the decor. Broad shelves held his teddy bears and other toys, and the furniture had been painted a bright blue to harmonize with the yellow and white wallpaper. She thought it a very pleasant room for a baby and imagined his pleasure at awakening in such a setting.

Unfortunately, Paul never had the opportunity; he refused even to sleep in it. Sylvia had scarcely placed him in his newly painted crib when he began to scream, pleading to be picked up. Gary was working at night, leaving Sylvia alone with Paul and Thor, their German Shepherd, so the baby slept in the room with her. Had Thor had his way, he would have too. As it was, the dog lay across the entrance to Sylvia's bedroom.

Sylvia lacked the energy to really focus on her apprehension about the house. Every day it seemed she felt a little worse. One afternoon when she'd finished her school day and brought Paul home from his babysitter's, she felt totally exhausted. Wearily, she placed the child in his playpen and entered the kitchen intending to fix dinner. Without warning, a wave of dizziness overcame her. It was the last thing that Sylvia remembered.

Just how long she lay unconscious she never knew. An angry, unsympathetic Gary aroused her when he came home for a dinner break. The next day Sylvia was too ill to go to work. "A little rest is all I need," she told Gary. "I'll go tomorrow." But when tomorrow came, she was even weaker. For ten days she lay on the couch, so ill that even the effort of moving her head brought on a violent wave of nausea.

Realizing at last that rest alone wasn't going to cure her, Sylvia asked a neighbor to drive her to the doctor. The physician, an old friend, rose to his feet, greeting her warmly as she entered his private office.

Sinking into the chair opposite him, she forced herself to smile back. It was reassuring to see a face she'd known since childhood.

But the doctor was anything but reassured by the sight of her. "What's the matter?" he asked.

She tried to joke. "I don't know, Jim. I seem to be developing a color scheme all my own."

"What do you mean?"

"Well," Sylvia replied, hesitating, "my urine is black and my you know what is white. Oh, yes, my eyes. Did you notice, they're turning yellow."

She was still speaking as he reached for the phone and dialed. "Emergency coming in," he informed someone on the other end. There were a few words that she didn't catch, then he hung up.

"What about me?" she asked, hurt and annoyed that his mind was on another patient.

"I'm afraid you're the emergency."

Sylvia was admitted to the hospital within an hour. By the time that day had ended, she'd been examined by five different physicians. Their diagnosis was acute hepatitis. At first she was too euphoric to worry. They'd given her a shot to control the nausea, and, for the first time in what seemed like weeks, her stomach was calm. But in the days that followed her body heat became unbearable and most of her skin surface was raw from scratching herself. "Bile salts coming to the surface," a nurse explained. Sylvia had never heard of bile salts; she knew only that she was in agony.

Learning that an operation was scheduled, she asked Francine, "Am I going to die?"

"Not now, too many things are planned for you," was the answer.

Sylvia wanted to cry at the prospect of more work, more unhappiness, more pain. Death had seemed a merciful release.

The surgery lasted for nearly five hours. A portion of Sylvia's liver, intestinal tract, and gallbladder were removed. She awoke suddenly in agonizing pain. No medication seemed to work. She began to pray, her eyes focused on the light above the bed. Then, sensing a presence, Sylvia turned her head warily, wondering what they were going to do to her next.

There beside her was Grandma Ada. "Is it really you?" she whispered, her voice hoarse from the tubes that had been inserted during the operation.

"Of course it is, sugar heart. Did you think I'd let you go through this alone?"

"Grandma, I can't stand the pain."

"It will be all right now. They've found the right medicine for you. It's on the way."

"I've made so many mistakes, nothing really turned out the way I intended. I have so much to tell you."

"You will one day, you will," Ada assured. Just then, the nurse entered the room and approached the bed.

"My grandmother's here," Sylvia informed her.

"No one's allowed in here," the nurse said, leaning forward to take Sylvia's pulse.

"You don't understand, my grandmother's dead."

"Of course she is," the nurse agreed, giving Sylvia's arm a little pat.

"She doesn't believe me, Grandma."

"Of course I believe you," the nurse placated her.

"Just close your eyes," Ada soothed. "Everything's going to be fine."

Sylvia awakened back in her hospital room. Bill was crying, Celeste was wringing her hands, Gary was staring out the window. Sylvia turned to Sharon, who was sitting beside the bed. "I just saw Grandma." The four of them looked away, looked at each other, looked everywhere but at Sylvia. "Really, I saw her. I even talked with her," Sylvia insisted, frustrated that they didn't believe her. In reality, they had taken the incident as a sign that she was dying. They were certain that Ada had come for her.

Seven days passed and Sylvia was still hooked up to the machines. Not even her stomach functioned without a tube while another apparatus drained the bile from her body. Gary refused to come to the hospital; the smell disturbed him. It was Bill who came every day. Invariably, he arrived just as Sylvia was vomiting. Joking, he accused her of saving it up for him, but it was obvious that he was very frightened. His little girl was growing weaker every day.

Alone in her hospital room, Sylvia thought about her

situation. How wonderful it would be to just slip away to wherever Grandma was. The thought of death had never frightened her and now the prospect seemed utter bliss— until she thought of Paul. If she died, he would be left with Gary, who'd never wanted him. She thought, too, of Francine and her continuing insistence that they had a job to do. Whatever it was, Sylvia realized that she would have to get on with it, and that meant getting well.

Gingerly, Sylvia reached for a spoonful of Jell-O. She took a bite, then realized what an exercise in futility that was. What nourishment was there with everything going out the stomach tube? Later, when the doctor came by on his rounds, she demanded that he remove the tubes immediately.

"Now Sylvia, you have to have patience," he said, attempting to soothe her.

"If I'm any more patient, I'll be dead. I'm never going to get well if everything that goes in goes right out of me," she argued. Then she threatened, "If you don't pull these tubes out, I will." The tubes were removed, all but the one that extracted bile. Almost immediately, Sylvia felt herself growing stronger.

One afternoon, as she continued to improve dramatically, Sylvia heard the nurses talking about a patient who had no visitors. Sylvia decided to pay a "call." She wheeled herself down the long hallway, carrying her bile tube and bottle with her.

Pausing in the doorway to catch her breath, she was struck by a flame of bright red hair flowing across a pillow. "Hello, I'm Sylvia," she introduced herself, pushing the wheelchair forward.

The woman turned feebly. Her face, nearly as pale as the bed linen, was quite beautiful. "I'm Maureen," she replied. Her smile was touchingly eager.

Soon Sylvia learned that Maureen was only a year older

than she. Maureen had a husband, but he'd left her. She also had four children and a mother who resented having to care for them while her daughter was hospitalized.

"The nurse told me you're here for a lung operation," Sylvia ventured.

"Yes, one of them's gone. They're going to fix the other today."

Sylvia knew almost instantly how the operation would turn out; it was very clear that she'd come to this room for a purpose. Wheeling herself up to the bed, she took Maureen's hand. They talked for hours, Sylvia sharing the wisdom that she'd received over the years from Francine.

"It's so scary to think of dying," Maureen confided. "Are *you* ever afraid?"

"No, no, not at all. I'm really not, because I know what the other side holds for me," Sylvia explained. She paused and said, "It's something to look forward to, not to fear."

"You mean it really is heaven?"

"Heaven, paradise, nirvana—whatever you want to call it. All those words describe the same place, our eternal home where our experience of God and each other isn't restricted to the limitations of time and space. Beauty and wisdom are there waiting for us. All the pain and trauma of life fades to a pale memory. The degree of our soul's perfection is the badge of having lived." Sylvia's love for Francine had never been greater.

"I'm not sure my soul's all that perfect," Maureen confided.

"Well, neither's mine; but we're both doing our best—aren't we?"

Maureen nodded. "I've tried very hard."

"That's what it's all about, trying hard and learning lessons. We'll have lessons to learn on the other side as well, but there won't be pain attached to it. You can believe me, dying is like going home—only better, much more wonderful than any home in this world could ever be."

"Oh, that sounds so nice," Maureen sighed, leaning back. She seemed to have attained almost total peace.

"Yes, it *is* nice, it's really heavenly—so heavenly that if we could envision it clearly, we'd all want to go there now rather than wait. The problem wouldn't be feeling frightened at leaving this world, but rather sad at the pain of having to stay here knowing there's something so much better beyond."

Sylvia stayed with Maureen throughout the preoperative procedure, holding her hand until the attendants came to take her to surgery. As they were wheeling her out, Maureen gave Sylvia's hand a final squeeze. "I'll never forget you," she promised. "When you get to the other side, I'll be there to welcome you."

Eventually, Sylvia went home, but, despite Gary's impatience, she wasn't allowed to work for a month. At night, she and Paul were alone in the house. Paul still refused to sleep in his room. Even Thor refused to go upstairs, raising his hackles and digging in his paws whenever anyone tried to force him.

It was lonely now; Gary came home only for meals and to sleep. One evening Sharon came to spend the night. The two young women had just finished dinner when Sylvia entered the bedroom she shared with Gary to get the television log. Confronting her on the wall above the dresser were three mysterious markings: a blue glowing star, a half moon, and an insignia that looked like a swastika. Despite her familiarity with metaphysical phenomena, there was a sense of menace about the apparitions that caused Sylvia to panic. Her frightened scream brought Sharon running.

Summoning their courage, the two women approached

the markings. "Maybe they're reflections from something," Sharon suggested. She seemed somehow less shaken than Sylvia.

"From what?" Sylvia wondered, glancing about. To accommodate Gary's need to sleep days, they'd installed black night shades that kept out all light.

Thoroughly mystified, Sylvia and Sharon hung blankets over the night shades and stuffed the door jambs. The markings remained. In the daylight, they would vanish only to return the following night.

"Why don't you ask Francine about it?" Sharon suggested.

Sylvia laughed nervously. Why hadn't *she* thought of that?

"Your house is built on an Indian burial ground," Francine told her. "They resent your intrusion. You will not be happy in this house."

Sylvia doubted that she would be happy anywhere, but nevertheless told Gary what her guide had said.

"That's crazy," he insisted. "The marks—if they exist—have to be lights from somewhere, and the burial ground stuff sounds silly. I don't believe it."

Sylvia knew that the swastika was an Indian symbol. The next day at the library she was able to find an old land grant and map. So near as she could determine, their house actually was built squarely on an old Indian burial ground.

"Well, so what?" Gary responded when she told him. "Don't you suppose somebody's buried everywhere?"

"Maybe," she conceded, "but the point is, we're not meant to be here." Gary returned to his television program, effectively tuning her out.

Then the events leading to their exodus came in rapid succession. A few days later a tornado hit their house— and only theirs. It was the only structure touched. Fortunately, the damage was slight. "Don't you think someone or something might be trying to tell us—" Sylvia suggested, then stopped. Gary had elaborately turned his back and returned to his newspaper.

Then, a few days later, Gary was suspended from the police force. Before long he found a position as an insurance adjuster, but showed little aptitude for the job. A month later, on the very day that he was discharged, the house caught fire without any apparent cause. There was some damage, but as with the tornado, no one was injured. The next day Thor was literally thrown through the screen door. There was no discernible cause. That night, Gary placed a long-distance call to Sunnyvale, California.

His old friend, Don, had left the force the same time he had and was currently working for the Sunnyvale Police Department. "Come on out," he suggested. "I know I can get you on here. Put Sylvia on," he said in conclusion. "Barbara wants to talk to her."

"It's wonderful in California—no more snow to shovel," Barbara enthused.

"What do you think?" Gary surprised Sylvia by asking after she'd hung up.

"I think I'd go anywhere to get out of this house."

"Okay!" he yelled.

Six weeks later they'd sold the house and most of their furniture, had shipped the dog, and were heading west. Only once, thinking of the family and friends she was leaving behind, did Sylvia turn and look over her shoulder. But on the far horizon she saw the swirling cone of a tornado. That was enough. There was no more turning back.

CHAPTER SIX

Nirvana

"YOUR marriage—it won't last much longer. There's another woman coming into your life, a somewhat older woman. She'll be much better for you."

It was Francine speaking. Sylvia, oblivious to the handsome, dark-haired man sitting opposite her, was literally entranced.

Later, returning to consciousness, the medium was aware of the man's thoughtful manner. "Was it bad news?" she asked anxiously.

"Don't you know? Don't you remember anything?" he asked as he studied her curiously.

"Never. Once I've asked Francine to come in—once she takes over—I'm out of it. It may be my lips moving, but I have no idea what they're saying. Whatever is I or me or Sylvia is out in space somewhere. Then Francine leaves and I come 'home' again."

"Aren't you afraid of not coming back?"

"No, I'm really not. Francine's my best friend, she'd never do anything to hurt or frighten me. Besides, the last thing she'd ever want would be to be stuck in *this* world."

"I don't understand how you do it."

"Nor do I, really. It's something that just happened one day and then over the years I've developed shortcuts. But I'm more interested in you. You're sad about something that Francine told you."

"Yes," he admitted. "It's my marriage. You—Francine—said it was going to end."

"Francine reads blueprints, but of course there's such a thing as free will. It's possible that what she sees is simply a strain on your marriage, a problem area that you can work on."

"I'm not sure I want to."

Sylvia smiled sympathetically. "It's that bad?"

He nodded and then sat silently for a few moments. Sylvia felt his depression and empathized. She thought of numerous platitudes but none seemed appropriate. The baby within her kicked. In less than six weeks he'd be making his presence felt in the world. Sylvia pulled herself heavily to her feet.

Her subject rose, too. Dal Brown, at twenty-two, was the youngest captain in the history of the Stanford University Fire Department. Sylvia thought him the handsomest man she'd ever met. What a pity he was so unhappy. Was this the natural condition of life?

"Francine doesn't give information that you're not meant to hear," she reminded him. "But what you decide to do about it—that's your choice."

"But you're psychic too, aren't you? It isn't just Francine?" he persisted.

"That's right."

"Well, can't *you* tell me something? Francine mentioned another woman."

Sylvia strained inwardly, but surprisingly, her mind's screen was blank. Then, very slowly, a woman appeared next to Dal. "Yes, there is someone. She's tall, red-haired . . . That's funny!"

"What's funny?" Her subject was intense, eager.

"Not amusing, but strange. I can't seem to see her face. I always see faces—why can't I see hers?"

"Francine said she'd be good for me," he ventured.

"Yes, she will be, I can tell that. She'll be very good; and her boys, you'll like them, too."

"Her boys?"

"Yes, I see two of them." Sylvia paused, searching for more. "I just can't see her face . . . but there's a business, some kind of business, you'll go into it together. It will make you both very happy."

"Anything else?"

Confused, Sylvia shook her head. "I'm sorry, but that's all I'm getting."

The door opened and Gary looked in. "You two about done? It's getting late."

"We're finished," Sylvia replied. She reached for her coat. Outside in the living room, the other firemen were waiting to say goodnight. She'd read for each of them that evening. On the way home, Gary quizzed her. "How did it go?"

"You know better than that," she answered wearily. "How should I know? It was a trance, not a reading. You'd have a better idea than I. You saw each of them as they came out."

"They really seemed impressed, every one of them. You were the hit of the evening. The guys really go for all that spook stuff."

She smiled wryly at the note of surprise in his voice. It was always like that. Sylvia repressed a sigh. Lack of recognition in her own home was the least of her problems. Gary's pleasure at the indirect admiration her abilities brought him was one of the few pluses in their troubled relationship.

Her mind moved, as it often did, over the two years since their arrival in California. The move had changed nothing. Gary's bad luck had continued. Don Crowther had been unable to find him a place on the Sunnyvale Police Force. For a while it was Sylvia who had supported the family, this time by teaching at St. Albert the Great Elementary School in Palo Alto.

Then, one morning six weeks after their arrival, Sylvia opened the door to confront the smiling faces of Bill, Celeste, and Sharon. Bill had resigned the vice presidency of his company, and the Shoemakers had sold their home and moved to California, arriving without warning to surprise their daughter. Sylvia's feelings were mixed. Though she'd often felt guilt and concern at leaving them behind in Kansas City, there'd been a sense of relief at being removed from their problems. Now the respite the separation had brought was over. For more than a year both familes lived together, Sylvia frantically juggling the demands of husband, child, parents, students, striving as always to please them all. The Shoemakers moved out of Sylvia and Gary's home only when the two families purchased a duplex and settled down to live side by side.

But there had been one reprieve for Sylvia. On one evening every week she escaped into another world. Sylvia had enrolled in the English literature master's program at San Francisco University. Challenging as undergraduate college life had been to the young girl, the woman was even more stimulated by graduate work. As time passed, Sylvia's originality and enthusiasm were noted by her creative writing professor, Bob Williams. Soon the two were enjoying vigorous literary debates at a campus coffee shop. "*Ulysses* has been my favorite assignment thus far," she surprised him by announcing one night.

"Most students find it difficult, hard to relate to."

"Oh, no!" she exclaimed. "I know exactly what Joyce's talking about. That part about the tower in the tarot deck—it's as though he were talking to me."

"Really?" Williams leaned forward, intrigued. "Do you mean you actually understand the tarot cards?"

"Yes, of course. Each card represents some aspect of

our journey on this earth. The whole wonderful deck is a kind of compendium of knowledge, a symbolic record of human experience."

"And the tower?"

"Well, the traditional meaning is a sudden conflict or catastrophe, but, as an upset of the existing order of things—the old notions—it could bring enlightenment as well."

"You sound like a fortune-teller! Do you read the cards?"

"I love the tarot, those symbols have so much beauty and truth in them, but I don't need cards to know what's going to happen."

Williams nearly dropped his coffee cup. "You mean to tell me that you're really psychic?"

"It's more like I'd rather *not* tell you that I'm psychic. Back home in Kansas City everyone knew me and no one cared that I was different. People just took it for granted that 'Sylvia knew things.' I'm afraid it wouldn't be like that here. When we moved to California—when I began a new life—I made up my mind not to tell anyone." Sylvia felt a growing sense of apprehension as she studied the professor's expression closely. "Now don't *you* tell."

The professor promised to keep her confidence, but pressed for details, and soon Sylvia found herself telling him all about Francine. "Could you come to class an hour early and do a reading for me?" he urged.

Reluctantly, Sylvia agreed. A few days later she arrived at the promised time and found not only Williams waiting eagerly, but two of his friends.

The following week, when the creative writing class concluded its survey of *Ulysses*, Williams announced that Mrs. Dufresne would discuss tarot symbolism and give a demonstration of divination. Sylvia was furious with him, but there were fifty pairs of eyes trained on her. The perennial people-pleaser found it impossible to say no.

Later, it became obvious that those fifty people had told at least fifty more. Sylvia very soon found herself speaking to other classes, to women's clubs, even to business organizations. Inevitably, the demand for individual readings grew to be tremendous, but somehow Sylvia managed to accommodate everyone. Nothing terrible happened. Friends and acquaintances continued to accept her, and, as many appeared to benefit from the information she was able to give them, Sylvia concluded that perhaps Bob Williams had been somehow meant to blow her cover.

During the next months, adjustments were made and a new life pattern emerged. Gary eventually found a job with the fire department at Stanford University. The Dufresnes and the Shoemakers had bought their duplex together. Sylvia was teaching at Presentation High School in San Jose and looking forward to the birth of her second child. She hoped that the baby's arrival might herald a reconciliation with Gary.

Christopher Michael Dufresne was born on February 19, 1966. He was a healthy infant from the beginning and Sylvia was spared the crushing depression that had followed the birth of her first child. She adjusted easily to the necessary changes in her routine, mothering, teaching, attending classes and giving readings. She loved every minute of her busy days.

But there was no improvement in the relationship with Gary. Their continued inability to achieve sexual intimacy left her lonely and frustrated. She tried to compensate for her own imagined shortcomings by working harder, doing and earning more. Months passed and finally years. Then one day it became suddenly clear. She could *never* do enough to please her husband. It was a "no win" situation.

Sylvia then and there took stock of her life. At thirty-five, she could make it on her own. She *was* making it on her own—both economically and emotionally. What was the point of continuing in a marriage that served only to undermine her self-esteem?

That was the day Sylvia walked out.

In the weeks that followed, the ringing phone usually meant the Shoemakers were calling to urge their little girl to come home to them. "How can I?" she asked. "There's only a thin wall between you and Gary." Actually, Sylvia was grateful for the excuse. Bill and Celeste had been devastated by her sudden decision. Having their daughter and grandsons practically in the same house with them had been a dream come true. They refused to believe that anything could be seriously wrong between Sylvia and Gary and took every opportunity to importune her to return to him and to them.

Sylvia, Paul, and Chris had taken "temporary" refuge with the newly married Sharon, but as their stay stretched on and on, nerves grew frayed. Sylvia spent every possible moment searching for an affordable home that would allow children, have a fenced area for her boys to play in, and was near a baby-sitter. "Is it possible?" she asked Francine in desperation.

"The perfect home is waiting for you," Francine reassured her, but would say no more. Sylvia was beginning to suspect that her guide was referring to the other side.

One morning, as she returned from a frantic round of house hunting, she was met by a curious Sharon. "A very interesting-sounding man called."

"Well, if it wasn't Daddy, it has to be someone wanting a reading. I just can't take time to do any more until I'm settled. You were supposed to explain that to people," she reminded her sister.

"Well, it's sort of like that, but all this fellow wanted was to tell you that you were right on. He *did* break up with his wife."

"Who was it?" Sylvia asked, sinking wearily into a chair.

Why were people always so surprised when she was right, she wondered absently.

Sharon consulted a pad of notepaper by the phone. "He said his name was Dal—Dal Brown."

"Dal Brown!" Sylvia perked up immediately. "Dal Brown's separated? Did he leave a number?"

Sharon handed her the paper. "Who is he?"

"Oh, he's quite a guy." Sylvia studied the number a moment, then quickly picked up the phone and dialed. Soon they were talking.

"I always thought you were the perfect happily married couple," Dal said. "Gary used to give me advice on how to treat Margaret."

"No wonder your marriage failed!" Sylvia exclaimed, finding herself laughing for the first time in weeks. "Why don't we get together, maybe have dinner?"

"I don't think that would be right. I only left yesterday," Dal explained.

"Then how about an affair?"

Sylvia was joking, of course. Or was she? Sylvia and Dal went out that evening and never separated. It was the kind of union she'd always dreamed of, a true merging of souls as well as bodies. The following day Sylvia and her two small boys moved into Dal's new apartment.

Gary was furious and so were Celeste and Bill. While married to Gary, Sylvia still belonged to her parents. Dal was an unknown, someone who might somehow estrange her from them. They fought the match in every way possible, even going so far as to back Gary in an attempt to have the children taken from her. For one of the few times in her life, Sylvia defied her parents, standing firm in her resolve to remain with Dal.

On January 4, 1972—the very first day they were both legally free—Sylvia and Dal were married in Reno, Nevada. It was a joyous occasion, different in every respect from her first marriage. Sylvia could scarcely believe her ears when Dal announced, "You've been working too hard for too long. It's time that someone took care of *you* for a change."

At his insistence, Sylvia remained at home for one year. For the first time in her adult life she had time and space for herself, precious hours in which to think and to read, to both cultivate friends and enjoy solitude. Best of all, there was the opportunity to really get to know her children.

Toward the end of that year, Dal and Sylvia attended a lecture by a well-known San Francisco area psychic. As the evening progressed, Dal, always sensitive to Sylvia's moods, was aware of her growing tension. When the psychic asked for questions from the floor, Sylvia repeatedly raised her hand, but, to her growing frustration, she was never recognized.

Finally the demonstration ended and, as the Browns joined the others filing out of the auditorium, Dal asked, "What did you think?"

"I thought it was awful, really awful!"

"But she seemed to be on target."

"Yes," Sylvia agreed. "Most of the time I think she was, but you can not just leave people dangling like that."

"What do you mean?" he asked, puzzled.

"Oh, there were so many times. That woman, for instance, the one who asked if she and her husband had a chance of making their marriage work."

"You mean the plump blonde woman whose husband had been her son in a previous life?"

"That's the one. The medium made it seem absolutely hopeless. You can't just take someone out of an audience and dump on them like that."

"I seem to remember Francine giving me a little bad news," he reminded her.

Sylvia grinned. "As I understand it, she also gave you a little ray of hope."

"She did indeed," Dal agreed as he slid his arm around his wife.

"I'm serious, Dal."

"I'm serious, too. Here's a coffee shop. Shall we go in and have some coffee—or maybe tonight you'd like something a little stronger?"

"Don't you think I've spirits enough?"

"Coffee, then," he agreed, opening the door for her. Later, after they'd ordered, Dal pressed her further. "Don't you believe a medium should give a negative message if she gets it?"

"Of course I do. I believe I wouldn't get the information in the first place if I weren't supposed to pass it on, but I also believe that a medium has a responsibility. Sometimes counseling is required. Besides, just because the woman's husband was her son in one life doesn't mean that they can't work it out as man and wife in this one. It simply means that there's a problem area that needs to be allowed for and worked around. The medium might have given her a little advice on that. Instead, she left her feeling that her marriage was hopeless."

"Have you ever considered being a medium?"

"Really, Dal!" Sylvia stared at him in shocked exasperation. "What do you think I've been doing all my life?"

"I mean full time."

Her annoyance faded instantly as she grasped his meaning. Reaching across the table, Sylvia caressed Dal's hand tenderly. "That's impossible," she reminded him. "This year has been wonderful, but we both know it's time for me to go back to work."

"Couldn't doing readings *be* your work?"

"You don't mean charge for it!" Sylvia exclaimed. She set her coffee cup down with a heavy clunk.

"Why not?" he challenged her. "How many times have you said that psychic ability is no different from any other gift? Don't you think that writers or artists or cooks get paid for their talents? Why should mediums be any different?"

Sylvia was shocked. "But all these years I've never thought of charging," she protested.

"You've been marvelously generous with your time and talent—as you are with everything—but if you were to work full time at it, you'd *have* to charge."

She shook her head, dismissing the idea. "Teaching's my career. I've spent years training for it."

"Not as many as you've spent with Francine," he reminded her. "That woman we heard tonight just looked up from a dishpan one day and decided she was psychic. Do you imagine that she has anything near the track record that you have? You've been psychic all your life."

"It's impossible, Dal. I don't want to talk about it."

He agreeably changed the subject. They spoke no more about professional mediumship, but Sylvia was awake half the night thinking about it. In the morning it was she who brought up the subject. "Perhaps doing readings is simply another form of teaching," she ventured.

"Of course it is," he agreed. "You're actually teaching survival phenomena—showing people that there really is life after death."

"That's true," she agreed, "but I'd like to do more than teach it. I'd like to *prove* the survival of the human spirit. I'd like to do research."

"It would take an organization to do that, a foundation."

"Couldn't we become a foundation?"

Dal was silent, considering her eager face. "Why not? Why not!" he exclaimed at last, pulling her into his arms. "A foundation has to start somewhere."

CHAPTER SEVEN

The Other Side

THE Nirvana Foundation began with a small ad in the classified section. It read:

HUSBAND AND WIFE OFFERING CLASSES IN
PSYCHIC DEVELOPMENT

Twenty-two people showed up for the first class in the Browns' tiny San Jose apartment. Those twenty-two told another twenty-two and soon there wasn't room for them all. Somehow, Sylvia and Dal managed to scrape together enough money to rent a small storefront office. Her mind still very much on soul survival research, Sylvia named their enterprise "Nirvana," which means enlightenment or "the way." Determined to have a nonprofit foundation, the couple took out a twenty-four-hundred-dollar loan to cover legal expenses.

Sylvia was concerned with credibility. "I don't want anyone thinking this is some fly-by-night outfit," she explained. "Madame Lazonga, I'm not."

"There really is no way to certify a psychic," their attorney reminded them. "The only 'proof' will be your reputation." Sylvia nodded, certain at last that she was doing the right thing.

Almost immediately, that confidence was vindicated. People began to clamor for private readings. The office couldn't accommodate them all. In those early days, Sylvia charged five dollars and used tarot cards. People didn't always realize that the cards were merely a means of altering consciousness and achieving focus. At one session, Sylvia told a client that she had a throat problem. "Yes, you're right," the woman responded, "but where's the sore throat card?" Before long, Sylvia realized that she no longer needed the cards; she could confront her clients' problems head-on.

Though most of her time was spent giving readings, Sylvia's true focus remained on research. On a spring evening soon after the foundation was formed, a small group gathered to attend Sylvia's first open trance. Every person had at least one question to ask Francine.

The evening began as Sylvia made herself comfortable on the couch. Dal sat beside her, acting as a kind of protective buffer against sudden shocks, noises, or other disturbances, for Sylvia was quite literally "out" when Francine was "in." A loud noise occurring just as Francine was entering or vacating Sylvia could be dangerous to Sylvia. Dal began to count, "One thousand and ten, one thousand and nine, one thousand and eight, one thousand and seven . . ." Slowly, almost imperceptibly, Sylvia's face began to change. Her features somehow seemed to broaden and the "doe" eyes which are almost a Sylvia Brown trademark became hooded and more penetrating.

Slowly, cautiously, a young woman barely out of her teens edged forward. "Can you describe yourself?" she asked the spirit guide.

"Yes."

There was a low chuckle at the literal reply. "*Will* you describe yourself?"

So Francine, the entity who'd first appeared to a frightened child so many years before, described herself to the eager group and then went on to tell them that her information came from three major sources—Askashic records, individual spirit guides, and messages from the Godhead.

"The Askashic records are actually God's memory," she told them. "They are stored in a kind of library. There, all of the events of each individual's life are continually being recorded. It's like an epic motion picture in which everything that happens—past, present, and future—is depicted.

"Secondly, everyone has a spirit guide who is fully aware of the blueprint his or her person reflects. I am able to consult with that guide for detailed personal information." Francine reminded the audience, "The spirit guide is one's most intimate friend and companion on the earth plane. The guide's knowledge of a subject's motivations, percep- tions, and life is total. Churches sometimes call these beings 'guardian angels.'

"Information from the third source—the Godhead— comes in different forms," Francine continued matter-of- factly. "Every entity on the other side has complete com- munion with God. His presence is felt in a very tangible way by each soul. When I need information to guide Syl- via, I go to special groups of entities who speak for God with great knowledge and spirituality. But at other times I may simply pray directly to God for guidance—and He always answers. This type of information is known as 'in- fused knowledge.' It is available to all who ask."

The group digested this for a moment and then another woman spoke. "But how does infused knowledge work and what exactly is a spirit guide? What are *you*, Francine?"

"Infused knowledge is information that comes directly from the Holy Spirit. It's placed directly into the mind without the aid of any of the senses. It's an immediate acquisition of knowledge that you simply know without knowing how you know it. This information is to be shared with others—otherwise, God would not have given it to you.

"A spirit guide is simply an entity—just like you. I am

an entity just like you. My job and the job of all other spirit guides is to help those on earth to perfect themselves, as others have in turn helped us. No doubt many of you in this room will one day choose to be spirit guides when you make your transition to the other side."

A white-haired man in his late seventies asked, "Just what is the other side?"

Francine paused, as though searching for words. "It's simply another dimension," she replied at last in a soft voice so different from Sylvia's deep, husky tone. "It's paradise, it's heaven, it's the ultimate reality of existence. It is the living world, yours is moribund by comparison. You reside in a temporary state of unreality. The puny lifespan of one hundred years is a tiny drop in the great sea of eternity."

Once she had warmed to her subject, Francine's persona became more apparent. Though totally different from Sylvia's ebullient candor, her voice rang with quiet conviction. "Most of us reside on your plane of existence at one time or other in one or more lives in order to experience negativity. There is no negativity on the other side nor, for that matter, in the true reality of any existence. But since negativity is part of knowledge, and since the whole purpose of creation is to garner knowledge and experience, almost all of God's creations choose at some time to come to earth as part of our continuing education.

"In other words," Francine said becoming noticeably more intense, "the true reality of existence is in another higher-frequency dimension that is called 'the other side.' That dimension—which is beyond the realm of the five senses—is where we reside for eternity, except for our brief sojourns to planes of unreality. We live in these planes temporarily to experience negativity for the evolvement of our souls. The other side is our—and your—*real* home."

The older man, obviously pleased by the answer, persisted. "Just where is the other side?" he inquired.

Many now leaned forward intently, for it was a question puzzling everyone.

"It's right here," Francine surprised them by saying. "The other side is superimposed on your plane, but it is approximately three feet higher. This is the reason that those of you who have seen 'ghosts' or 'spirits' often see them floating slightly above ground level. Your plane and that of the other side share the same space. It is only because of the higher vibrational frequency of our matter that you are unable to see or perceive our existence. You are like 'ghosts' to us as well, but by concentrating, we're able to activate our senses to a keener pitch in order to bring you into clear focus.

"Because the laws of physics are different on the other side, we have more space in which to live. Without losing volume or size, hundreds of persons may be comfortable in a nine-by-twelve-foot room. Our physical laws allow us to do this without becoming microscopic because space on our plane is entirely different from yours. Consequently, we have more entities on our plane—approximately six billion—but we also have much more space and are not in the least crowded. This applies as well to land, bodies of water, and all material things."

As though anticipating the next question, Francine continued. "If you can imagine the most beautiful thing you have ever seen and multiply it a hundred times, then you might be close to the beauty of the other side. The colors are brighter, the flowers are more gorgeous and far larger than on your plane. All the beauties of nature exist here— mountains, seashores, lakes, trees. All the animals that you have on earth exist here as well, except that here they are friendly with each other. There is no aggression or hostility.

"It might be interesting for you to know that the pets which reside on your plane come to the other side when they die. If you have loved a dog or cat, it will be waiting for you when you come home. My dear Sylvia has a large area in which all the pets she has gathered throughout her incarnations live. When she comes home there will be a big reunion.

"We have beautiful fountains and plazas, courtyards and parks, as well as gardens and meditation areas. Though our architecture is predominantly classic Greek or Roman, we have areas that cater especially to an entity's fondness for a special lifestyle—a castle, an Elizabethan cottage, a log cabin, or a hacienda."

A teenage boy who was sitting on the floor near Sylvia moved a little closer. "Are there other inhabited planets?" he asked.

"There are millions of planets like yours on which entities in a variety of sizes and shapes exist," she told him. "Like your planet they also have an 'other side.' There are millions of 'other sides' and each is a duplication of beauty like the one for the planet Earth. We all exist in the same dimension and can travel back and forth at will."

The boy sat quietly for a moment, imagining the possibilities of what Francine had said, and then asked another question. "Do we each have a body on the other side?"

"You most certainly do," Francine assured him, and you and only you select it. You can choose from all the physical attributes that you'd like to have—your hair, weight, height, features, eye color, everything."

A smartly dressed woman in her late thirties spoke next. "What other abilities do we have on the other side that we don't have here?"

"There are three major areas," Francine explained. "Entities on the other side are able to communicate telepathically and generally do this when conversing in small groups. But with larger gatherings—in order to avoid confusion—we use verbal communication. Although all languages are used from time to time, our main language is Aramaic. We have selected Aramaic because it is ancient and simple, yet descriptive.

"We also have the ability to bilocate. Perhaps we want to visit someone or someplace and still continue our work. We then concentrate on being in that other place. The shift is accomplished easily and many entities choose to appear in several places at once for purposes of assistance. Our Lord, Jesus Christ, can appear in millions of places when needed.

"All knowledge is open to us. We not only have memories of what we have learned on earth as well as here, but we have access to the Askashic records which contain all knowledge—past, present, and future—for the planet that you call Earth."

The questioner's fingers moved rapidly as she jotted all this down in a small notebook. Then the woman looked up, a puzzled expression on her face. "Do we keep our earth identity on the other side? I'm rather attached to mine."

"Yes," Francine reassured her. "Your personality—your individuality—is a composite of all your experiences, whether they were gained on the other side or on Earth. Your experiences, whether good or bad, influence you as a person. If you have lived in various locales around the world in past lives, the experiences you garnered contribute toward the personality you have today in your present life.

"When you get to the other side, your personality remains the same but functions at an optimum. Imagine yourself at the happiest period of your life, with your personality at its peak, exuding charm and happiness. Then take this feeling and magnify it one hundred times and you will get an indication of how your personality works all the time on the other side."

"But what about the people we don't like on this planet?" someone asked. "Will we suddenly like everyone when we get to the other side?"

It was a question that struck a responsive chord among everyone in the room. Francine responded without hesitation. "Likes and dislikes are a part of an individual's personality and are directly attributable to one's own experiences. If one individual does not care for another, it is usually due to the fact that the individual's experience with her or him has been negative. Dislike is not created existentially in an entity. It must be formed from one's own experience with the object of that dislike.

"If, for example, an individual has a strong dislike, perhaps even a hate for an uncle, this may have been created by the behavior of the uncle toward that person as a child. Perhaps the dislike is fully justified. On your plane, feelings may be altered by forgiveness or may remain unchanged. But on the other side, our awareness may open up. We understand why the uncle treated us badly. Perhaps it was caused by too much pressure on the uncle or possibly it was a learning experience needed by the soul. Whatever the reason, this knowledge gives us an entirely different outlook. We love all the souls of creation because each is a part of God, just as we are.

"Perhaps in some cases we don't desire intimacy with a person, but we still love that individual's soul. Each and every entity has a choice to associate with those it chooses. All of us have our close friends—that is part of the personality—but I know of no one who hates or even dislikes another entity on our plane. There is just too much love and harmony.

"The main reason for that love and harmony is the lack of ego involvement. There is no competition on the other side. Everyone works together for the common good. Pride and jealousy no longer have meaning for us because we have learned that the true purpose of our existence is to love and obtain knowledge about God. It is easy to help one another on our side because there is no negativity to confuse us."

There was a low murmur as people discussed this answer and then a man spoke up. "But what about *this* world?" he asked. "We've got so much negativity to contend with. Is it okay to get angry at people or situations?"

"It is not only permissible but *right*," Francine surprised them by saying. "You are not on the other side yet; you're still human. Anger is inverted depression. It is inverted because you cannot stand up and be who you are because you are afraid of peer group disapproval. And yet who do you admire in life? Who but the eccentric, the person who does what he or she pleases.

"No one can drain you. You allow yourself to be drained. It is because you are angry but feel that you cannot say what you would like to say. Instead you put up with someone's maudlin whining and wonder why you are exhausted. You lack the intestinal fortitude to stand up and say, 'I do not like this. This bothers me. I do not need it.' Would this be hurting the other person? No, it is hurting you *not* to say it.

"If you have spent a year or two with an individual and the relationship does not improve, you are wasting your time by allowing it to continue. You have every right to get away from a constant, painful situation. You do not have to wait till you get to the other side to be happy, but do know that the happiness you enjoy here is as nothing compared to what you will experience on the other side."

Another teenager seated on the floor, this one a girl, moved in closer. "What about social activities, Francine? Do you have parties on the other side?"

"Indeed yes," the girl was assured. "We have innumerable social activities, so many and so varied as to appeal to every taste. There is music and dancing in large ballrooms, there are lectures and debates on almost any subject held in large forums, there are art shows and galleries featuring every kind of art, there are sports events and science exhibits, fashion and design shows, everything that you can imagine. Whether one wants to view these things as a spectator or be a direct participant is up to the individual.

"But in addition to the large events, there are smaller gatherings, such as poetry readings and chamber concerts. There are also spas to visit and wilderness areas to explore—swimming, sailing, mountain climbing, tennis. Though eating isn't necessary, some people enjoy gourmet cooking and nearly everyone likes to invite others in for a get-together.

"When you come home to the other side you will find yourself hard-pressed not to engage in some sort of social activity frequently. Although you certainly don't have to participate, most so choose. I myself am what you might call a party girl. I love parties and dancing and go regularly to those to which I am invited. Sylvia sometimes jokes about the fact that when I am not around her, I am off at some party. I do love them, as most entities do."

It took a while for the group to digest that answer. It was so different from the traditional view of "heaven." Finally, it was the teenager's pretty blonde mother who broke the silence. "What can anyone do for all eternity?"

It actually seemed that Francine was surprised by the question. "You work, you socialize, you learn and you enjoy your existence," she answered. "It is interesting to note here that we are all thirty years of age on the other side. This is a perfect age, as you have the ideal combination of youth and maturity. The Elders have the appearance of being older, but that is due to their projection of wisdom and learning. Our sense of time is so different from yours—your lifetime is only a few minutes to us—and our lives are so full that eternity exists for us as a state of bliss."

A man in his late twenties spoke next. He was seated toward the back of the room, his hand clasping that of a woman seated beside him. "Do you have marriage on the other side?" he asked.

"Since we live in some cases many lives on your earth plane, we may have had, in various incarnations, several husbands or wives. It is not likely that we would want to be permanently united with so many. Indeed, we might choose to merge with one soulmate."

The sweet-faced young woman seated beside him leaned forward and asked, "What does the term 'soulmate' really mean?"

"Its meaning is often misunderstood by those on your plane," Francine admitted. "Let me begin by explaining the difference between 'soulmate' and 'kindred soul.'

"When we were created by the Godhead, we were basically and intrinsically whole—for the most part. I say for the most part because a soulmate is actually the other half of oneself—unless you were created as a single unattached being for the purpose of experiencing that single state. The soulmate comes together with you when you have both determined that the time is right for this duality relationship to occur. It is, in essence, a marriage for all eternity.

"Soulmates exist singularly until they have reached their own chosen level of experience and evolvement. Once they have more or less gone through their training, they come together. This can take eons, depending on the individuals involved. Some have already gone through this process of learning and are now together, while others are still evolving. When the time is right, they will come together.

"An entity may or may not have a soulmate, depending upon whether or not that entity is a singular creation or whether or not it has reached the time of coming together on this plane.

"Kindred souls are souls that have a very deep platonic love for each other. Most of us have literally millions of kindred souls that we can relate to, but we will usually have only one soulmate. If, for example, you have a deep, loving friendship in this life with someone, chances are very probably that you are kindred souls on the other side. All of your close friends on the other side are kindred souls. We have a kind of soul merging here that is non-sexual. It's an act in which one entity enters another and experiences a merging of mind and body that is very intense and pleasurable. The mental high is indescribable."

The woman hesitated a moment. Her pale face colored slightly as she asked, "Is there sex on the other side?" Everyone in the room reacted in varying degrees, some leaning forward eagerly, others stirring uncomfortably, a few laughing. Sylvia remained supine on the couch; only her lips moved as Francine's voice came through.

"Yes, we do have sex on the other side. We call it merging. It is difficult to explain because it is both spiritual and physical. There is nothing that compares with it on your plane. If you take the most intense and pleasurable orgasm that you have ever had and multiply it by a hundred, you might come close to what an orgasm is on our side. Our orgasms also last much longer. Imagine an orgasm on your plane that lasted for several hours.

"Although merging generally involves soulmates, single entities or those who have not yet come together with their soulmates may also choose to participate in merging with another entity. You must understand that there is no moral judgment for this act between nonsoulmates because they always come together with the purest intent: love.

"Morality as you know it does not exist on the other side. There is no such thing as bad because all entities are loving and without ego involvement. We have no need for laws.

"On our side soulmates come together in a traditional way. The male entity proposes to the female entity. If she is inclined and if both are at the level of evolvement that they want to reach, she accepts and they go to the Council to receive a blessing. Once this is given, they begin to live together. However, this does not diminsh any of their prior social customs, activities, or friends. Many soulmates live very happily doing things together while others may prefer to pursue their own interests in a singular manner for a portion of their time. Either lifestyle is commonly practiced."

The group was quiet for a few moments, each person occupied with private thoughts. Finally, a portly, gray-haired man asked the next question. "Do you work on the other side?"

"All entities work on the other side, but the word *work* is probably misleading to you because it sounds like drudgery. We all enjoy working very much in our chosen fields of endeavor. It's not like on your plane, where you work to feed, clothe, and house yourselves. We do not work to survive. We work because we enjoy it and gain knowledge from it.

"It is interesting," Francine continued, "that all the knowledge garnered on your earth plane, new inventions as well as rediscoveries of ancient knowledge, has been developed first on our side. This knowledge is gained from our research and then introduced into your plane by implantation into the brain of a researcher, scientist, philosopher, or whatever. All inventions, all medical cures, all new scientific discoveries are transmitted from our plane to yours for your benefit and use. Even such things as music, art, and new designs are implanted by us into individuals on your plane.

"Since time as you know it does not exist on our plane, we have plenty of leisure to pursue hobbies. Each of us enjoys at least one in addition to 'work.'

"Of course, we do keep track of time in your dimension so that we can understand world events on your side as well as what is going on in a specific individual's life. We need an awareness of your time in order to monitor your progress.

"When your loved ones pass over into our plane they often have a difficult time relating to your problems because of the time factor. They realize almost immediately that you will soon be with them and your problems seem very short-lived and insignificant. You may have years to live, but to your loved ones it seems only a few minutes before you will be home again, safe and secure.

"It is like a child of yours who pricks a finger with a thorn. You may be sympathetic, but you cannot get too concerned because you know the pain will soon go away and the child will be laughing again. This is the reason that a 'control' like myself has to go through such extensive training. Without it we would not be able to relate to your human experience. We forget about negativity on the other side—*your* side—and must reintroduce ourselves to it in order to work with a medium—Sylvia, for example.

"So do not feel upset if some dear loved one passes over and you do not feel his or her presence or receive some form of communication from beyond the grave. This person may be very involved in his or her own work and just waiting for the short period to pass until you come home."

A small woman in her early forties seated in the back of the room spoke next, asking, "If life is forever, why do we have such a fear of death?"

"You come into life with a subconscious memory that life is forever, but that memory soon is blocked by the nature of the life experience on your plane, which forces you to only consciously remember what you have experienced there. It is somewhat like this: Have you ever lived in a house that you were afraid to give up because you might not find another? Or have you gone on a long trip and thought, Will I ever get back to the old house? Or perhaps, on returning from another trip, you said to yourself, I had forgotten just how very good home is.

"That is very much what life on your plane is like. Don't you often feel sorrow at the realization that your body separates you from others? Don't you long at times to pull another person into yourself? Don't you often feel a sense of isolation? Once you begin to recognize and understand this principle, the fear of death will dissipate; and, when you pass over, the memory will burst upon you at that very moment. Then your soul will breathe a sigh of relief: That is all over and I am home."

The woman sighed audibly. "That does sound so nice, but I wonder, then, what is the purpose of it all? What is the purpose of living?"

"You are all messengers from God sent here to carry His word. But that message is coded and you must break the code yourself. It is true that God exists within you, but *all* of you are a part of Him as well. You will live forever, you have lived forever, and no one will ever be lost or diminished.

"Spirituality means, in essence, to find yourself, to find the God within and without, and to fight the battle against negativity. You see, even if just one of you will go out and light the way for another, some of the grayness will be banished. This is how negativity is fought, and it only takes a handful of you to accomplish a great deal.

"Each of you is here to evolve your soul. You have chosen to experience life in order to perfect more rapidly. You are an evolving part of God, perfecting one aspect to Him. God experiences through His creations.

"Start looking at life as something you must survive. It can be fun at times, but it can also be very tedious. Think of life as a school in which the dormitory serves poor food and there is no worthwhile transportation. Yes, it will help if you maintain a sense of humor about it all."

The older, gray-haired man laughed heartily with the others, but then questioned, "Why does God need me for learning? Can't He experience directly?"

"God, having all knowledge, needed to experience His knowledge. From this need arose all creation, a manifestation of God's power and intellect. Every facet of God can be found in His work. The perfect love of our Father became so great that it began to multiply itself and in so doing created all of us. Since that time we have been the direct experiencing, emotional side of Him.

"You are, literally, a part of God. As such, anything you experience is also experienced by Him. If you are in some difficulty, then God too experiences it. If you discover a joyous facet of life, then God too is there.

"It is true that God needs us to experience. Yet it is more correct to say that God *is* us, and thereby He does experience directly. But He does have experience over and above what we have. This is true because he has *all* knowledge, whereas we have very little by comparison. For example, say someone in your life has all knowledge of biology—they have read everything in the world about it. Then say they have no practical experience of biology, they lack the sense and feel, the experience of that science. By knowledge alone they can experience much, but not as much as if by experiencing biology directly. People are the sensing, feeling aspect of God's awareness. Yet because of his boundless knowledge, His perception of our experience is far greater than our own.

The man nodded, considering what Francine had said, then asked, "What signposts mark our path? How can we know when we're on the right track?"

"Self-acceptance and self-knowledge indicate that you are doing well. You will feel good about yourself. You will begin to realize that, regardless of what adversity you may go through, you can handle it spiritually. Circumstances may temporarily derail you, but there is always an

Even as a youngster, Sylvia knew things that other children did not. It was her maternal grandmother, Ada Coil (far right, below) who reassured the gifted young psychic and taught her how to work with her talent.

Sylvia's parents, Celeste (above) and Bill (right), were not always comfortable with their daughter's abilities. Even when Sylvia was small her mother retreated from her daughter's problems. Handsome, charming Bill (shown here with Sylvia at a high school father-daughter dance) encouraged Sylvia to engage in the social activities of "normal" women.

Sharon, Sylvia's younger sister, shown here at age nine in a photo booth with Sylvia, might never have reached that age if her big sister hadn't seen the dire threat to the infant girl's life.

By her senior year in high school (when this photo was taken) Sylvia's abilities were well known among her friends, but in college she would meet many people who were much less accepting.

Sylvia had bad luck with two homes. The tract house she and her first husband bought in Kansas City (left) could have been the model for the home in *Poltergeist*. The duplex she moved to in Sunnyvale, California, was supposed to be a dream house, but it soon became the repository of tremendous amounts of bad energy.

Sylvia's two sons: Chris, at eight months, and Paul, at five and a half years.

Psychic Ghost Hunter

plus Whatever Happened To Peter Max?

PM magazine

Sylvia has become a regular on Bay Area television shows over the years, and has recently been making return appearances on several Los Angeles shows as well.

SYLVIA'S SCORECARD

Psychic Sylvia Brown reviews last year's predictions and predicts for 1987.

people are talking

TOMORROW 10 AM

5

(Photo courtesy of
Arthur Mintz Photography,
Saratoga, California)

Chris Dufresne, Sylvia's son and a practicing psychic himself, has inherited Sylvia's gift.

One of Sylvia's many appearances on A.M./LA with Steve Edwards and Tawny Little.

The sprawling Winchester Mystery House in San Jose, California, provided fertile ground for some of Sylvia's early research into hauntings and apparitions. (Photo courtesy Winchester Mystery House)

After a series of reports that the Toys R Us in Sunnyvale, California, was haunted, a local TV station asked Sylvia to investigate. This photograph, taken just at the moment Sylvia felt she made contact with the spirit, shows an unexplained image of a man in the aisle (upper left). This photo used infrared film; another photo using normal film showed no one in this aisle. (Photo courtesy William E. Tidwell)

The Church of Novus Spiritus has grown into a large and significant organization. Here, Sylvia speaks to the congregation at the weekly service. (Photo courtesy Robert Laws)

inner faith and glow that draw you back to inner peace. It is an intuitive awareness that you are okay, as well as a love for yourself that is totally necessary. This will in turn bring a heightened understanding and sensitivity that will enable you to hear guides and feel their presence."

The whole room was still while each person mentally evaluated his or her progress. At last, a woman in her late twenties spoke. "Do you have houses on the other side?" she wondered.

Francine paused a moment, as though considering how best to answer the question. "Many of us prefer communal apartments—I do—because of the opportunity for social life. But others, particularly many of the soulmates, may prefer houses. These houses may be of any kind of architecture. Some will be elaborately furnished and others are very simple. Some entities choose to build their houses in the conventional way, enjoying the act of construction. There are carpenters and other artisans on our side who can do anything.

"Others create a building merely by thinking it into being. For example, suppose we want to construct a new forum. After the site is selected, several architects outline the contours of the building using their thoughts alone. If you were watching this being done, you would actually see lines forming in midair, almost as though the architect were drawing them on a draftsman's table. Sometimes the builder will outline the contour of the building, decide he doesn't care for it, and then erase the 'energy' lines and start anew.

"Once the style of the building is established, other entities gather and together they create the substance of the building—the walls, roof, windows, interior furnishing. All of this is done through concentrated thought processes that condense the real matter.

"Sometimes we follow the same type of process in determining our appearance. If, say after several eons, you wish to change your appearance, you merely concentrate on the changes you want to make and, as easily as that, change from dark hair and brown eyes to being a blue-eyed blonde."

The woman nodded, acknowledging the answer, then decided to venture another question. "Do you have some form of government on the other side?"

"No," Francine answered. "We do not have a government *per se*, but we do have a hierarchy. This is in the form of a Council of Elders. We also have, in a decreasing order of responsibility, archetypes, controls, seventh-level entities, sixth-level, fifth-level entities, fourth-level, and so forth.

"The Elders are old souls who have a very wise and beautiful Godlike love for everyone. Much information comes from the Elders. You might call them spokesmen for the Godhead, at least in a spoken form. They are humanoid and—unlike the rest of us—choose, with their white hair and beards, the appearance of age. The Elders are wise and loving and their knowledge is vast. If any edict is to be pronounced, they perform that function.

"Archetypes are also humanoids in form but are very different from any of the other entitites on our side. They all look alike, almost like android robots in human form. Another difference is that they all communicate telepathically with each other, but do not communicate with others. That doesn't mean that they do not respond to us—they do: But it is like dealing with a deaf-mute. They are all very bright and actually seem to glow with an energy that no one else has. Many times, if you look at one for an extended period, your eyes react as if you had a flashbulb go off in front of you. The Elders say that the purpose of the archetypes is protection for those on your plane as well as ours. They are very powerful creatures, and controls and spirit guides use them frequently to help guide their earthly protégés. In your Bible, they have been called archangels, and because of their brightness and energy they have sometimes been seen by those in your dimension and confused with an apparition of Christ. Not too much is known about them. They are still something of a mystery even to us, but the love and protection they have given to us is not.

"Controls are advanced and evolved entities who act like spirit guides but perform additional duties, such as communicating with your plane through mediums in various ways. This communication can take the form of verbalization through a medium who is in a trance, channeling verbalization through a clairaudient medium, both of which I do. Or it can involve manifesting physical phenomena through a physical medium and channeling energy through a psychic healer. All of these functions of the control require extensive training because, if they are not done properly, the medium could be seriously injured. It takes many of your years of training to become a control, while most everyone performs the function of being a spirit guide at one time or another.

"For the purpose of categorizing and organizing groups of entities according to their experience and vocation, seven levels have evolved on the other side. These are not levels of spiritual evolvement, but only of experience.

"The first and second levels are levels of orientation—temporary states experienced by entities that have just passed over from your plane to mine.

"The third level embraces all entities who choose a simple lifestyle. These are entities who choose to work with animal husbandry, with agriculture, or with a craft such as carpentry.

"Fourth-level entities select more aesthetic pursuits, such as art, writing, sculpture, or music.

"Those entities who are counselors in such areas as business, science, and medicine are in the fifth level.

"The sixth level comprises entities who are organizers, teachers, and philosophers.

"Seventh-level entities are those who choose to go back into the Godhead and therefore do not really reside on the other side for an extended period. I might add that very few entities choose the seventh level; those who do lose their individuality, since the energy of their creation is taken back into the Godhead. Those who do elect this level are very spiritual and evolved, for their love of God is so great that they wish to be absorbed back into Him.

"Because of the experience needed by managers in various types of vocational endeavor, the fifth and sixth levels take more responsibility and become heads of research projects and orientation centers and majordomos of large areas of residence on the other side.

"If one were to say we had a form of government, it would most likely resemble the pure form of the ancient Greek democracy. There is complete interaction with all on my side, and everyone has the power to act or contribute if they choose. As there is no ego involvement on the other side, everything functions with complete love and harmony and a desire to do the best both for each individual and for the whole.

"Regardless of what level we have chosen to live in, we are all a part of the same dimension. There are areas on my side in which all are predominantly on the same level, but that state is for convenience and lifestyle or vocational purpose. All levels are equal and are designated only by experience and vocation. Usually, the higher levels are chosen by entities who have more experience in life. They have usually been on the earth plane in more incarnations and so have gained more experience with negativity."

The teenage boy who'd spoken earlier raised his hand. "You don't have to do that," Dal reminded him. "You're not in school."

"I don't know," the youth responded. "Maybe I am,

but I sure like this kind of school better than my regular one. What is the purpose of negativity?" he asked Francine. "Why experience it at all?"

"While the other side is the home and true reality for us all, most who reside there choose to incarnate briefly to the earth plane in order to experience negativity and to learn how to deal with it. Since negativity is a part of knowledge, we would be incomplete without having experienced it.

"It is much easier to be positive in a perfect environment, so we come to test our mettle on your plane. It is something we undertake for our soul's evolvement."

"Can we see God or Christ on the other side?" It was the gray-haired woman speaking again.

"God is always present on our side, though not in a bodily form. His presence is so powerful that it is felt through every pore of one's being. He constantly communicates with all on the other side through mental infusion. That manifestation of the energy of His love is always there, but there is another way of communicating with Him. It is called going behind the seventh level and is in essence the energy of all the entitites who have chosen to go to the seventh level.

"Since all of us are a small portion of God's energy and contain a portion of His knowledge, the many entities who have chosen to go to the seventh level have magnified this force into a power that potentially contains all of His knowledge. It cannot be defined or described.

"Christ exists on our plane in bodily form and lives with his soulmate, Mary Magdalen. His power and goodness are constant as he walks and talks with entities on the other side. Since He can divide Himself and appear in many locations, there is ample opportunity for anyone to seek His counsel at any time. On some occasions he may be seated by a fountain in serious and loving conversation with one person while laughing happily with a group.

"Our Lord has a wonderful sense of humor and enjoys parties, yet remains the ultimate philosopher and counselor. His time is spent in simply being there for all who need Him."

The teenage girl who'd spoken earlier in the evening moved forward slightly, a shy smile on her face. "Would you tell us about your life on the other side, Francine?"

"Most of my time is taken up in guiding Sylvia and watching her loved ones. In addition, I spend some time researching for my communications to those of you on the earth plane to whom I speak through Sylvia's body in a trance session such as this. The rest of my time is spent like most entities in attendance at lectures, concerts, parties.

"I have a soulmate and his name is David. We love each other very much, but do not do everything together. We have our own individual interests as well as our shared ones. Sometimes, when David and I want to do something together, I ask Raheim—Dal Brown's control—to watch over Sylvia, but I am never away from her for long.

"Being the control for a medium such as Sylvia can be somewhat confining in comparison to my former lifestyle before becoming a control: But in the overall scheme of things this is very temporary. The span of Sylvia's life on the earth plane seems much longer to you than to us on the other side.

"I discuss my work with friends as much as possible and will often consult with Raheim, the Elders, and Christ about Sylvia and her life's work. I keep in touch with the latest developments in the arts and sciences on your plane in order to understand better the various forces that affect Sylvia's life as well as the lives of those who come to her for help.

"When I finish my job as Sylvia's control, I will go back to my normal, more relaxed lifestyle. I will return to my work at the orientation center where I help those who are making their transitions from your side to mine.

"I have chosen to evolve and perfect my soul by doing work on this plane rather than going into a great number of incarnations. My life as Iena was my first and last incarnation on your side. This method is slower, but what is the hurry? I have eternity."

Dal brushed a strand of Sylvia's hair back from her forehead. "This has been a long session. We don't want to tire Sylvia," he reminded the people. "Francine may have eternity, but Sylvia's a very busy lady with readings to do first thing tomorrow."

Gently he gave her the command to return to consciousness. Within instants Sylvia was Sylvia, sitting up, smiling, and joking. "Did Francine tell you who your prom date will be?" she asked the pretty girl seated on the floor before her.

"I forgot to ask. As a matter of fact, there are still a few other questions I'd like to ask some night."

"Only a few? What a lucky girl you are." The elderly man, her grandfather, had come forward to thank Sylvia. "I fear that most of us have many more questions. Isn't it lucky there's all eternity to work on them?"

CHAPTER EIGHT

The Reading Room

SYLVIA'S office was the best that she and Dal could afford, but it was awful. There were two tiny rooms—a minuscule waiting room and Sylvia's scarcely larger office.

She settled in early in the morning on June 11, 1974, placed a photograph of Grandma Ada on the desk before her, and sat back. Sylvia had anticipated a sense of pleasure at having her own office, but instead she had a feeling of mounting panic. The walls were closing in on her. I can't stand this a moment longer, she realized, I'm getting claustrophobia. She alleviated the problem with a quick trip to a nearby department store.

When Dal dropped by later that afternoon, he stopped short in amazement. "I didn't remember a window here," he said. Puzzled, he pulled the drapery cord. The drapes parted to reveal a blank wall.

"It makes me *feel* like there's a window," she explained.

Other problems weren't so easily resolved. The smell, for instance, at times seemed overwhelming. That week one of her first clients commented on the strong odor of Lysol.

"Well, yes, I suppose it is rather heavy," Sylvia admitted, "but I thought it was better than that other smell."

"Other smell?"

"Yes, can't you smell it? No matter how much Lysol I

spray around this place, I can't get rid of that urine smell. I just can't figure out where it's coming from."

The client, a heavy-set grandmother type, laughed. "Maybe you'd better pay some attention to *this* world, honey. Didn't you notice the diaper service next door?"

Sylvia laughed with her client, but later reflected. She was reminded of the ancient saying, "As above, so below." The universe was not about to allow her to become too spiritual. Like it or not, she was well grounded in the everyday world. But it went further than that. Now it seemed that all the factors that had clouded her life—her father's infidelities, her affair with Ski, her depression, illnesses, and unhappy marriage—had all been for a purpose. She had needed those experiences to give her greater empathy for all aspects of the human condition. She was not, she realized, a priestess dispassionately channeling from aloft. It might be a cliché to say, "I know where you're coming from"; but in Sylvia's case, it was true. Sylvia had been there too.

Not only could she read for her clients, she could feel their pain. This personal understanding would enable her to avoid the worst pitfall she'd observed in open readings where the medium dumped information with no apparent concern for any subtleties of feeling within the individual receiving it. Now, with so many total strangers coming into her life, it was a relief for Sylvia to realize that her hard-won empathy would enable her to heal rather than hurt.

Looking now at the woman before her, Sylvia "saw" a husband suffering with multiple sclerosis. Sylvia questioned her gently. "You know that your husband is seriously ill, don't you?" she asked.

The woman nodded her head and replied, "Yes."

As Sylvia probed psychically, she knew her client was ready for the whole truth. "He'll be gone in two years."

"That's why I came to see you," the woman replied. "I

wanted to know how long we have together. I want to arrange things so that we can make the most of it."

In those early days it was the money issue that troubled Sylvia the most. It had been one thing to accept money for teaching, a skill she'd spent years training to acquire; but doing readings was something else entirely. Sylvia had *always* been psychic; now it seemed she was suddenly being paid for simply being herself.

When Sylvia officially opened the doors of her storefront office at 249 East Campbell Avenue, her fee was seven dollars and fifty cents. The first week there were five clients, one of them an avowed skeptic. He sat in the slightly battered second-hand armchair across from Sylvia, his hands clenched into fists. As she talked, he shook his head violently.

"What's the matter?" Sylvia asked at last. "Does your neck hurt?"

"I'm shaking my head 'no.' You're totally off. That marriage stuff—forget it. I've parted company with one wife; there's no way that I'm going to go through that again."

"What do you mean 'no'?" she challenged him. "How can you shake your head 'no' when I'm talking about the future? If you could foretell the future you'd be sitting here and me there. Now let's get down to business. Who's this Penny person whom you call Puff?"

The identifying question stopped him cold—exactly what Sylvia had intended. Such statements about the present establish the medium's credibility to foresee the future, soothing and reassuring clients and allowing them to benefit from the reading. Some of Sylvia's early clients were so skeptical that she felt she was arm wrestling them into submission, but this enabled her to get on with the real business of finding helpful material.

The second week, there were thirty clients. One of them

was a small, rather thin woman in her late forties. Her face was tense, her manner anxious. She had barely seated herself before Sylvia got a picture of a young woman lying dead in a dark alley, her chest covered with blood.

If I receive the message, she's meant to hear it, Sylvia reminded herself, but her heart sank at the ordeal of describing her vision. "I see a young woman. She's thin with blonde hair," Sylvia began.

"Yes, yes," the older woman said, leaning forward, her hands pressing against the edge of Sylvia's desk.

"Her skin is rough, almost pockmarked," Sylvia continued. "She's off at a distance. In the east—a very large city."

"That's my daughter. I came to you about her. The last I knew she was in New York. Is she all right?"

Sylvia took a deep breath. "No, she's not all right. I have to tell you, she's going to die. In fact, she may even be dead now."

"Thank you," the woman responded, her voice soft, controlled. Her quiet dignity put Sylvia at ease. "It may surprise you to hear this, but I've known for a long time that my girl was headed for disaster. She's been involved with drugs since she was a teenager. She's mixed up in a drug ring, the Mafia's involved." The woman began to sob quietly. "There's nothing that I could do, nothing that anyone could do, but the waiting, the uncertainty, is so terrible. I imagine them hurting her, torturing her, and I feel such helplessness."

"No," Sylvia was relieved and happy to say. "It's not like that. It's very sudden, a gunshot wound. She may not even know what hit her."

"Thank you," the woman said again. She pulled herself wearily to her feet.

"Would you like—shall I try to see what else—" Sylvia began.

"No, perhaps I'll come back another time. This is

enough for now. Don't feel sad. You think you've given me bad news, but actually you've done me a favor. I don't have to be afraid any more, to dread any more. You've told me the worst and even that isn't as bad as it might have been."

Sylvia rose, crossing the small room in an instant, and opened the door for the woman. The two hugged briefly. "You've a wonderful gift, please don't stop using it," the woman urged and then turned and walked away. Sylvia closed the door softly behind her and leaned against it for a moment, certain at last that she had made the right decision. It was indeed time to come out of the closet.

Within a month it became clear that Sylvia not only needed more space but help as well. Bill quit his job and came to work at the Nirvana Foundation as office manager. Soon he was joined by Larry Beck, a student at San Jose University, who still assists with research. Before long, Larry's friend, Laurie Halseth, was a staff member as well.

One day Laurie approached Sylvia tentatively. "Do you think Larry and I will ever marry?"

"Yes, I know you will," Sylvia told her. "You two will marry, but it will only last five years. There's someone else out there for you—someone for Larry, too." (Actually, the Becks' marriage lasted five years and eleven days.)

Meanwhile, the Nirvana Foundation moved to larger quarters. The Goodwill sofa supported by bricks was replaced by a newer model. Sylvia raised her rates to fifteen dollars. Before long, another move was necessary, and then another. To cover the cost of her growing staff and activities, Sylvia's fees climbed to thirty dollars. Reflecting on the accounting, financial consulting, and law firms that shared the building with her, she thought sometimes of her former hippie neighbors and their blaring music.

Today the comfortably furnished Nirvana Foundation

occupies three thousand square feet and commands a view of the Santa Cruz Mountains. The full-time staff of fourteen includes Dal, who serves as business manager, Sylvia's son, Chris, who does readings, Sylvia's sister, Sharon, and Sharon's husband, Richard. A variety of classes and other services are regularly offered as well as an array of cassettes and booklets. But the focal point remains the reading room.

It was obvious to Sylvia from the beginning that with each client who came there she was essentially reading a blueprint. "Where does this come from?" she asked Francine.

"Each and every person creates his or her own blueprint from birth. Each person decides the kind of parents and childhood that he or she will have, the kind of marriage, career, health, death—"

"But why should anyone choose the awful things that so often happen?"

"Life's lessons are necessary. Only through adversity does one's soul progress. Think of it, Sylvia—what have you learned from the good things that have happened?"

Sylvia considered, then admitted the results weren't impressive. The hard times, however, had made her strong. She remembered vividly the dark days of her depression and the sense of accomplishment she'd felt when she thought, I made it, I may have shook a lot but at least I got up and brushed my hair and moved around and took care of Paul, I taught school, cooked for Gary, cleaned the house, all of it. Now, surely, those memories increased her rapport with clients facing the same kinds of problems. Because of her experiences, she was better able to help others and that, apparently, was *her* blueprint.

But there were some people that Sylvia could not help. One was Curtis Bitney.

Curtis had come into her life as a friend of her son, Chris. As a teenager, the activities of the Foundation were like food and drink to him. Attending his first open trance, Curtis had surprised everyone by greeting Francine as an old friend. While others remained in awe of the spirit, Curtis walked right up and sat down by the couch where Sylvia was lying entranced. "Hi, Francine," he greeted her cheerily. "How are you?"

"Very well, Curtis," she'd replied. "It's good to see you here."

Curtis was eager to learn everything about the supernatural. He participated in research projects, helping Sylvia in every way he could. He enrolled in her hypnosis class, hoping to learn past-life regression. One day as Sylvia looked at him seated in the front row, she had a terrifying vision of him lying dead on Highway 17, his smashed motorcycle beside him.

"This is important," she told him. "I don't want you riding your motorcycle on the freeway. Stay away from Highway 17. I mean it. Will you promise me?"

"Sure, sure," he agreed. Laughing, he looked away from her. Three days later he was dead. A car had sideswiped his motorcycle on Highway 17.

Sylvia was distraught. Why hadn't he heeded her warning? Bitterly, she thought of those who accused her of trying to control the lives of her clients through mediumship. It was impossible. Everyone fulfills the destiny they create themselves. For whatever reason, Curtis had programmed himself to die at that time in the exact manner that he had. Sometimes the blueprint was unalterable—she could not change it.

But on other occasions it seemed to Sylvia that she herself was part of the client's blueprint, that her message was meant to avert disaster. When Kent Herkenrath came to her for a reading early in 1979, she saw the wreckage of a plane and sensed it was in the Midwest some time in May. "Don't go flying off somewhere in May," she warned him.

"But that's exactly when I'll be returning from a business trip to Chicago," he told her. "I can't let something like this ruin my life."

"It's up to you, of course, but I see it very clearly. You're in an airport running for a plane. I wouldn't get on that plane if I were you."

Two months later, Herkenrath was in O'Hare Airport. He was late, hurrying to catch a plane back to San Jose. As he turned from the ticket counter, he glanced absently at the airline calendar. It was May. Sylvia's words flashed through his mind. Almost running, he approached the gate. Passengers were already boarding.

Herkenrath started to give his boarding pass to the agent and then pulled back. The man looked at him, puzzled. "Sorry, I guess I've changed my mind. I'll take a later plane," he mumbled, embarrassed, and he turned away.

That plane, an American Airlines DC-10, crashed shortly after takeoff killing 275 people. It was May 25, 1979.

Sylvia had thought often of the two men, the one who took her advice and lived, and the other who chose instead to die. Could it be, she wonders now, that for whatever reason, it was part of Kent Herkenrath's blueprint that he should come to her to receive a warning that would save his life?

Sylvia had been aware since girlhood of the existence of blueprints that guided the lives of most of her subjects. But now, as more and more people came to her, she realized that each particular script lacked one component.

"My life is a mess," each client would almost invariably insist. "Everything's wrong." But as Sylvia investigated psychically, she realized that it wasn't everything that was wrong, it was some *one* thing. And curiously, it was this one problem area that was usually the most difficult for her to read. As always, with one exception, the individual's life was psychically accessible to her, each aspect clearly delineated. Invariably, one area would be vague, the conclusion undecided. With some it would be finances, with others love, with still others a career.

Puzzled, she consulted Francine. "What does it mean?" she asked.

"Those areas—the vague, undecided ones—are option lines," the spirit guide explained. "Each individual, when deciding upon his or her blueprint, also selects an area to leave open. This is what makes life interesting."

Sylvia disagreed. "This" was what made life painful. All around her she saw sorrow and frustration. It became increasingly obvious to her that few people came to a psychic in a happy state. Most were battle scarred, so very tired. Sylvia came to feel that the reading room was a kind of "MASH" unit where she had to patch people up quickly and send them on their way because outside there were a hundred others waiting for help.

On the other hand, Sylvia's good friend, William Yabroff, an associate psychology professor at the University of Santa Clara, who'd begun working with her on psychic research, observed her remarkable process in action. Again and again Sylvia was able to penetrate to the heart of the problem almost instantly and was thus able to effect healings that might take a conventional therapist several years.

Now, as in the early days, much of Sylvia's work focuses on option lines. There are seven of them—health, career, spirituality, love, finance, social life, and family. Despite her avoidance of subjectivity, Sylvia came to realize almost immediately that her own option line was family. No matter how hard she has always tried it has been impossible to reconcile the members of her family to one another. Bill and Celeste continue to quarrel and Sylvia's sons, Paul and Chris, are not always the best of friends. Sylvia's continuing struggle is to please them all. It is an often-futile effort.

The difference today is that Sylvia is now aware of what is going on, aware that at one point at least she did have some choice in the matter. Sylvia elected while on the other side prior to this incarnation to confront family problems as her option line during this life. It is this realization that enables her to maintain her hard-won equilibrium. It's the helplessness, the sense of being a victim that makes life most difficult, she now concludes.

Early on, Sylvia noted that problems with option lines cause people to believe that their whole lives are in a shambles. "Everything's terrible," a client once complained to her.

She looked at the distinguished man in his late forties and shook her head. "No, it isn't," she surprised him by saying. "Your health is fine, so are your finances, your career," she ticked each area off on her fingers. "It's just your love life that's off—way off. You've chosen one young nymphette after another. Sooner or later you grow bored, the whole thing becomes disillusioning, and you become depressed. Or else the women leave you for someone younger, making you even more depressed."

"Yes, you're right," he admitted. "That does seem to be my pattern. Whichever way it goes I end up alone and feeling rotten. Maybe the rest of my life is pretty good, but what's the use of having the other things if there's no one to share them with? Why, I wonder, do I always meet the wrong women?"

"The room could be full of women and you would still choose the wrong ones—at least they're wrong for you if you truly want a lasting relationship."

"I do want that, I really do," he insisted. "I feel awful and I'm sick of it."

"Then program yourself," Sylvia advised him. "Decide what you really want in a woman. Write it down, if that makes it easier. Whatever you do, get really clear. 'I want a woman four years younger. I want someone with a good mind, a sense of humor, someone who is at ease with all types of people, someone warm and caring,' whatever it is that *you* really want in a woman. Make certain that you know what you really want, then go after it and don't accept substitutes. You are in control. You—are—not—a—victim. You don't have to go off with the next bimbo you see. You can really have the woman you want, the relationship you want, the life you want—*if* you decide to program yourself for it."

Sylvia found that this same type of advice worked well on other option line problems. A woman with terminal cancer literally turned her life around and three years later was living a healthy, normal life. A man on the verge of bankruptcy programmed his way to solvency.

An option line is literally an option. Often this fuzzy area seems to permeate one's whole life, but Sylvia feels that the healing process begins with identifying the central problem and deciding on remedial measures. One can either consciously decide to make positive changes with no waffling allowed, or one can elect to recognize the option line, realize that it was personally selected for a reason, and learn to live with it.

She herself has chosen the latter. By recognizing her family situation for the growth opportunity that it is, Sylvia has learned to flow with it. The frustration, the frantic desire to flail about, is gone, enabling her to get on with the business of life.

CHAPTER NINE

Haunting Expressions

WHEN Dr. Marshall Renbarger moved into a new office in San Jose early in 1975, he was delighted by the convenient Crown Avenue location. But then strange things started happening.

First he heard loud clanging church bells. But there was no church. Next, he began to sense that he was not alone when he was alone. Finally, there was the presence of strange dark-robed men gliding silently about his office.

When he discovered that no one else heard or saw the things that he was experiencing, Dr. Renbarger got concerned. "Maybe I'm going crazy," he confided to a friend. "Wait till I tell you what's happening around here."

The friend stopped him, "I'll be right over to see for myself."

Fortunately for Renbarger's peace of mind, his friend was Sylvia Brown, who was able immediately to tune into the situation.

Upon entering the office she was suddenly assailed by the smell of incense. "What are you burning?" she asked, "it's so strong." Renbarger looked at her in puzzled surprise. "Nothing," he replied. "Nothing at all."

As Sylvia looked about the office-waiting room, she began to see a series of scenes seemingly imposed over one other. She saw a steeple, then a bell. As she looked about her, the walls seemed to give way. There was a small baptismal font and, off to the side, a row of small cells in which she saw monks kneeling in prayer. Then, right before her eyes, another monk walked through Renbarger's waiting room ringing a small bell.

"What do you see?" the doctor gasped. "What are you looking at?"

"I know it sounds crazy, but there's a whole other world going on right here, right at the same time our world is going on. There's a kind of church here. It's very small, a chapel really."

"What does it look like?"

"It's very simple, primitive, *old*; I've never seen anything like it."

"Like a mission?" Renbarger ventured.

"Yes! That's it exactly. It's a tiny mission, a Spanish mission."

"And people?" he asked, almost whispering. "Do you see any people?"

"Yes, I see several monks. They're wearing long brown robes. They're very busy. They're all over the place performing all kinds of tasks. They seem so happy here."

"I certainly don't feel very happy sharing my office with a lot of dead people."

"You've nothing to fear from them, really," she assured him. Renbarger was doubtful, but the arrival of his first patient prevented any further conversation.

Sylvia went immediately to the library and then to the county recorder, where she found the verification she was seeking. During the early days of California, a Spanish chapel had stood on the site of Dr. Renbarger's office.

"I don't know if I want to hear this," Renbarger responded when she called him. "Is it better to be haunted than crazy?"

"Definitely," she assured him. "It's all very peaceful. The priests seem to have settled happily into their earthly routine, they don't want to leave it. You don't exist in their dimension, but of course, even if you did, they would never harm you."

Renbarger's experience brought another to Sylvia's mind—her own. The mellow vibes of the doctor's office were a far cry from the sinister aura that seemed to envelop the Missouri tract house where she'd lived some years before with Gary. How frightened she had been then, how helpless she had felt. But hadn't some of that been a reflection of her own emotional condition at the time?

Now that Sylvia's life was coming together with a happy marriage and a burgeoning career, she felt confident and eager, ready to take on a new area of paranormal research. Her foundation was already dedicated to documenting survival phenomena. Weren't ghosts and haunted houses merely another aspect of this?

Unlike most psychic researchers, Sylvia had access to an insider, a true expert. "Just what causes a haunting?" she asked Francine. "How does it come about?"

"Hauntings often are caused by earthbound spirits, entities who have a sense of unfinished business," her spirit guide replied. "The priests you saw are an example. They simply do not know that they are dead and so continue in their familiar rituals. In this case, the lives remembered are peaceful, happy ones, but that isn't true for all earthbound spirits. Often with others there is a sense of confusion or frustration. They seek a lost person or object, they attempt to right a wrong.

"But," she continued, "the phenomena that you call haunting may have another cause as well. Energy implants may also be responsible. Sometimes the energy is positive—happy times evoke a light, pleasurable ambience—but at other times the opposite is true."

Sylvia immediately thought of the house in Sunnyvale where she and Gary had lived until their separation. The duplex, still owned by her parents, had been the scene of so many angry battles when she and Gary lived there. In recent years her parents had rented it to a series of couples with disastrous results for the tenants' marriages. Now Bill and Celeste were considering its sale.

Many of the tenants had been newlyweds and all had initially seemed happy and affectionate. But no matter how blissful the couples appeared at first, the neighbors soon were complaining about the noise, shouting, and screaming coming from that half of the duplex. Violence occurred with almost every couple. The turnover was frequent and always for the same cause—divorce.

"I don't know what came over me," the man would almost always say, vainly trying to explain his brutal conduct. "It's so strange; he was never like that before," his wife would complain.

Surely, Sylvia reasoned now, there was something that could be done about it.

"It is time for you to do an exorcism," Francine surprised her by announcing.

Sylvia was shocked. She knew nothing about exorcisms, had no idea how to go about performing one.

"It is quite simple," Francine assured her. "Use a white candle, salt, and holy water. Encircle the house with the salt and seal each door and window with the water. Do this at night, lighting your way with a white candle."

Sylvia was dubious. "Where would I get holy water?"

"Make it yourself. Holy water is created by leaving ordinary water in the sunlight for three hours. Make the sign of the cross over it three times during that period."

Now Sylvia was even more dubious. It all sounded so hokey.

"It is *not* hokey," Francine assured her. "Such rituals have power because they are so very ancient. Just do as I tell you and you will see for yourself."

Reluctantly, Sylvia agreed. She realized that, if the exorcism was to be done at all, it should be attempted as soon as possible. Sylvia went alone very late at night, hoping that the tenants would be asleep. Happily, she noted that the house was dark. Getting out of the car as quietly as possible, she walked all around the building with her candle, stopping before each door and window to sprinkle salt and water.

At first Sylvia felt silly, but as she tuned into the vibrations of the house, she could feel the hostility and pain. Softly she prayed for peace, a peace that would heal not only the young couple sleeping inside, but the house itself.

As she knelt before the French doors and began to pour a line of salt across the doorstep, a window opened next door.

"What the hell are you doing?" a man demanded to know.

"Just killing snails." It was the best excuse she could think of. There were a few moments of silence that seemed like hours while Sylvia envisioned herself burned for witchcraft or at the very least roasted in the morning paper. Then the window was lowered. Slowly, softly, deliberately, Sylvia continued her work. When every opening had been carefully sealed, Sylvia walked back to her car and drove home.

To her very great relief, the exorcism was a success—completely so. No more violence, no more problems of any kind have been reported. The tenants are happy, the neighbors are happy. The trouble has dissipated as mysteriously as it began.

Whether caused by energy implants or earthbound spirits, the phenomena of haunting continued to absorb Sylvia. She was determined to seek out valid case histories and document them. Fortuitously, it wasn't necessary to look far. One of the most famous haunted houses in the world was located only a few miles from her home.

It was Sarah Winchester's famous mystery-shrouded mansion in San Jose, where every night is a veritable Halloween. An aura of dark foreboding surrounds the massive, sprawling structure; the towering spires, minarets, and cupolas stand dark and still, silhouetted against what always seems a glowering sky. Inside are trap doors, secret passageways, and doors that open into the air. The Gothic Victorian is a living monument to the dead. The legend of Sarah Winchester, who tried to shut out the grim realities of life and death, is everywhere.

The story of Sarah Winchester—possibly the most enigmatic woman in the history of the West—is as fascinating as the legend of the house itself. To the pioneers of the nineteenth century, the Winchester repeating rifle was the "gun that won the West." But to Sarah Pardee Winchester, heiress of the fortune of the Winchester Repeating Arms Company, the weapon was an instrument of doom and a portent of her ultimate destruction.

According to the story, Sarah, the widow of the rifle manufacturer's only son, was informed by a Boston medium that the spirits of all those killed by Winchester rifles—and most particularly the Indians—had placed a solemn curse upon her. The medium advised Sarah that she might escape the curse if she were to move West and build a house. As long as the building continued, she was advised, the vengeful spirits would be thwarted and Sarah would live.

The unhappy heiress obediently took her "blood money," as she called it, and moved to San Jose, where she purchased an eight-room farmhouse. She proceeded to remodel and expand literally as the spirits moved her. The construction project, begun in 1884, was to occupy the next thirty-eight years of her life and would ultimately employ hundreds of artisans working around the clock even on Sundays and holidays—all in accordance with the plans provided by Sarah Winchester's spirits.

Design conferences took place in the séance room,

where Sarah alone retired each night. In the morning the resulting plans, complete in every detail, were handed to the head carpenter. Hundreds of rooms were added, many of them only to be quickly ripped out to make way for new ideas from Mrs. Winchester's nocturnal architects. These spectral consultants were capricious and insatiable, demanding more and more rooms, balcony after balcony, chimney after chimney, tower after tower. The strange growth spread until it reached a distant barn, flowed around and adhered to it like a tumor, and finally engulfed it. Again and again observation towers rose, only to be choked by later construction.

Today, 160 rooms of this baffling labyrinth still stand, the survivors of an estimated 750 chambers interconnected by trick doors, self-intersecting balconies, and dead-end stairways. Literally miles of winding, twisting, bewildering corridors snake their way through the house. Many of the numerous secret passageways are concealed within the walls. Some end in closets, others in blank walls. The door from one was the rear wall of a walk-in icebox. The halls vary in width from two feet to regulation size, and some ceilings are so low that an average-size person must stoop to avoid bumping his head.

The explanation for all this is that the house was designed by ghosts for ghosts. If stories from that dominion are to be believed, spirits dearly love to vanish up chimneys. Sarah, always obliging, provided them with not one but forty-seven of these escape hatches. The séance room, where Sarah received her instructions, was off-limits to other humans. Those entering the forbidden sanctuary after her death were said to have found a small blue room furnished with only a cabinet, armchair, table, paper, and planchette board for automatic writing.

Despite her efforts to forestall it, death came to Sarah Winchester on September 5, 1922. Today, one can still see a row of half-driven nails where carpenters stopped when word came that the eighty-five-year-old recluse had died quietly in her sleep.

Of her twenty-one-million-dollar inheritance, the widow had spent at least five and a half million preinflation dollars to please her discarnate friends. Unless ghosts are unspeakable ingrates, Mrs. Winchester should have been well received.

But the story didn't end there. The mansion, known as "the world's largest, oddest dwelling" became a museum soon after Sarah's death. Next it was declared a California Historical Landmark and registered by the National Parks Service as a historical place. Rooms as well as the extensive gardens were refurbished. The maintenance of so large a place is continual. Today, most of the sounds heard in daylight hours are anything but spectral. In fact, the carpenter's hammer echoes just as it did during the mansion's heyday.

But there have been other sounds as well, strange puzzling sounds. Over the years tourists and staff have reported a variety of phenomena—chains rattling, whispers, footsteps, cold spots, filmy apparitions. To Sylvia, this Gothic-thriller brought-to-life was tailor made for investigation, an ideal spot in which to cut her teeth as a psychic investigator.

The thought was the act and she quickly arranged with the owners to spend a night in the house. There would be five in the party—Sylvia, Dal, a photographer, a foundation researcher, and this writer. Sylvia prepared for the event by not preparing, making it a point *not* to check into the history of the house or its inhabitants. At the time, Sylvia knew nothing of Sarah Winchester, other than that she had been the one-time owner of the mystery mansion.

Upon entering the house, Sylvia established her base camp in Sarah Winchester's séance room, one of the few with electricity. Because of its susceptibility to fire damage, very little of the gingerbread Gothic has been wired. The séance room, bare now with only a naked lightbulb dangling from the ceiling, soon seemed a snug haven to the team. The meandering passageways beyond, daunting enough in the daylight, were even more formidable in the dark. The tape recorder was unpacked along with twelve packages of tape still sealed in cellophane, six cameras, packaged film, and a metal detector.

From the séance room, the small party made forays into other parts of the house. Each member of the group felt sudden gusts of icy wind and cold spots for which there was no discernible reason. Once they were startled by moving lights for which they could not account, a kind of psychedelic light show which exploded out of nowhere only to disappear again. In Sarah Winchester's bedroom, while seated in total darkness, the party's resolve was tested by the sudden appearance of two great angry red globes that confronted them and then seemed to explode before their eyes, finally disintegrating into blackness.

Sylvia was the only one to hear organ music. The next day, however, when the tapes made that night were played back, the others heard the sounds as well. This seemed particularly important when it was uncovered in subsequent research that Sarah Winchester had loved to play the organ and reportedly had done so all night long when arthritic pains kept her sleepless.

As the rest of the group sat on the floor of the bedroom, clutching clipboards and cameras, Sylvia whispered a description of a couple watching from the doorway. During the thirty-eight years that Sarah Winchester resided in the "mystery house," her servants and other employees remained fiercely loyal, protecting her privacy and defending her every eccentricity. They described her as strong-minded and firm, but always fair and kind. Each was well paid and often rewarded with lifetime pensions or gifts of real estate.

In death, it would appear that Sarah received the same attention. "The man and woman I see are dressed in turn-of-the-century clothing," Sylvia explained. "The woman—her name's Maria—is Spanish-looking. She keeps wiping her hands on her apron. The man beside her has red hair. He's wearing overalls with a red kerchief around his neck. There's a big black dog with them, a labrador. They're caretakers. Their attitude isn't quite menacing, but they are watching us very carefully, suspiciously. They don't like strangers in their house. They don't like *us* here. They want us to leave."

As the night wore on the frightening sense of being observed did not diminish. Sylvia and her companions sat for about an hour watching a ghostly shadow play across the dark walls. Each of them tried to explain the spectral light show in earthly terms. Moonlight? There was no moon. Passing cars?

At times, the tension was almost unbearable. It was a very long night.

It had been an eerie initiation into what would become a sideline as a kind of ghost-chaser and exorcist. The following day Sylvia and her research team learned that Sarah Winchester's reclusive nature had even barred Teddy Roosevelt when he came to call. It appeared now that the tormented woman had moved on, no doubt finding on the other side the peace that had eluded her here.

For whatever reasons, the caretakers had remained behind, guarding the house in death as they had in life. The present owners find some advantage in preserving the house's "haunted" reputation, but Sylvia feels concern over the spectral pair, locked as they are in a lonely vigil. She has returned to the Winchester Mystery House several times specifically to speak with Sarah's caretakers. She has hoped to communicate to them that they are dead and to encourage them to follow their earthly mistress into the light, where they can get on with the work of fulfilling their own destinies. But they remain steadfast in their determination to stay with the house. On one occasion, a TV cameraman who'd accompanied Sylvia was able to photograph an apparition walking back and forth before the second-story window.

Since that cold January night in the early days of 1976, Sylvia's first trip to Winchester Mystery House, her field trips have taken her to many bizarre locations. One investigation brought her to California's Mother Lode country to investigate a murder committed more than a hundred years ago. Robert Chalmers, the merchant prince of the Gold Rush capital, was not only a member of the State Legislature but also a prizewinning vintner. His beautiful wife, Louise, with her easy elegance and proud, imperious ways, was the undisputed social leader of the area.

At the apex of their success, this pair of high rollers constructed a four-story mansion that was to be a mecca for the Mother Lode elite. Among the attractions of their "Vineyard House" was a ninety-foot ballroom and a music room.

But Robert Chalmers's pleasure was brief. Soon after completion of the showplace in 1878, his manner began to change. The former orator now spoke in whispers. Seeing a grave being dug in the cemetery across the street, he walked over and lay down to see if it would fit him. Soon, according to Louise, he was a raving maniac whom she was forced to chain in the cellar of their home. It was said that she came down often to taunt him, standing always just beyond his frenzied grasp. Chalmers's misery lasted for nearly three years. Then in 1881 he died under mysterious circumstances. Some said Louise had poisoned him, though no one could say for sure.

Visiting the scene of the tragedy a hundred years later, Sylvia was able to tune into both spirits. The sad truth was that Robert Chalmers had literally starved himself to death because he feared that Louise might kill him. "I meant him no harm," the spectral Louise insisted. "I only did what I had to do to protect him. If he'd been free he might have killed himself or someone else."

Another memorable investigation occurred at a nude beach resort in northern California. Even on a sunny day the place looked like a setting for a Gothic horror story. Coast Road winds its way through deserted stretches of hills and sea. On the November weekday the Nirvana research team visited, there was very little traffic.

A dirt road wound downward from the highway, twisting and turning around rolling moundlike hills. As Sylvia approached the isolated farmhouse that served as an office, she felt that she had stepped back in time a hundred years. If ever a house looked haunted, this one did. To Sylvia, the tall two-story structure seemed like some lonely sentinel, a mute survivor of penetrating fog and sea gales. But of what else, she wondered.

Ralph Edwards met the team at the gate. He was a tall, rangy man with a taciturn manner. "I hear you have a ghost," Sylvia greeted him.

"Better talk to my wife."

"You mean you never saw it?"

"I didn't say that." He turned back to his gardening.

Kathy Edwards proved the opposite of her laconic husband. She was full of stories—all of them frightening. "Things are relatively quiet now—those footsteps, they aren't much. They happen so often, Ralph wouldn't get any rest at night if he ran down to check every time we heard them. And the doors slamming by themselves, that's nothing. They do it most every day. My perfume bottles dance around a lot and we hear the sound of crystal shattering but never find anything broken.

"But when the girls were living at home, that's when the house was really active. My daughters used to have a terrible time at night. Something seemed determined to shake them right out of their beds. Sometimes they'd make up beds on the floor thinking they'd get away from it, but there was no escape. Every time they'd pull up the covers something would yank them away. I remember Ronda was working as a medical secretary—a really demanding job that kept her very busy. Sometimes I'd hear her pleading with the bed to let her sleep.

"My son, Roger, didn't believe his sisters, so one night he slept in Ronda's bed. Nothing happened and he soon was asleep. Then in the middle of the night he awakened thinking an earthquake had hit. The bed was shaking so violently that it seemed to leap right off the floor.

"Since the girls married and moved away, whatever it is seems to have shifted its attention to the first floor. People just won't stay overnight in this house. Our last guest was several years ago. A young relative sleeping on the couch was awakened by a rooster crowing. He could see its outline perched on the arm of the couch at his feet. But when he turned on the light nothing was there."

The Edwardses have never kept chickens.

One night, Kathy said, Ralph's Navy picture flew off the living room wall and sailed five feet before crashing to the ground. The force of the crash was so great that some of the glass splinters are still imbedded in the wood. The nail that had secured the picture remains in the wall.

"If you think any of this is funny, don't laugh too loud," Kathy advised. "I told a visitor about our ghost once and he laughed at me. That skepticism didn't amuse whatever lives here one bit. Suddenly a drawer opened by itself and a baby shoe flew out and hit him on the side of the head. That stopped his laughing in a hurry."

On Thanksgiving Day of 1975, Kathy Edwards was just opening the refrigerator door when a large plant left its standard and flew toward her—a distance of some twelve feet. Her daughter prevented a serious injury by grasping the heavy pot in midair. But the mess could not be avoided. The plant and dirt that had been in the pot crashed against Kathy and splattered the inside of the refrigerator. No fruit salad served at that holiday dinner!

Ronda was the target of another attack that occurred one evening with nine people present. A glass of wine sitting on the piano flew through the air and deliberately poured itself down the front of the young woman's de-colleté dress.

Sylvia had listened in silence as her senses tuned into the vibrations of the house. "You feel a heaviness in your chest at night, don't you, Ralph?"

"Yes." He nodded.

She continued, "Things move around in this house. They seem to get lost, disappear for no apparent reason."

"They sure do," Kathy agreed. "The first year we lived here, we were ready for the divorce court. I thought he'd taken things; he thought I had. Now I know that neither of us had. It was someone else, something else. Once I had a letter to deliver for one of the campers. It disappeared right out of my hand and appeared a day later in a laundry bag."

"I see an older man," Sylvia said. "He's wearing a rain-coat and hat. I feel dampness, rain, mist. I think he was a sea captain. He walks about the grounds. In his life he killed an intruder. He doesn't like company even now."

Excitedly Kathy explained that she'd found an old rain slicker and cap hanging on a hook on the back porch when they moved into the house. "At least a dozen people a year tell me they've seen an old man in a raincoat. I wonder sometimes if it couldn't be the sea captain who built this house in 1857."

"Yes," Sylvia agreed as she nodded, "I feel that it was." She was quiet a moment and then added, "The people who lived here before were an angry, unhappy family. There was a lot of hatred, a lot of unresolved problems. I see unhappy young people . . . a beautiful young girl

. . . blood. There was a stabbing here. There were evil acts committed in the past."

Kathy gasped. "A young girl did disappear mysteriously while visiting her uncle, who owned the place. That was in the very early 1900s. No one ever heard from her again. But a few years ago, when Ralph and I decided to put in a barbecue pit, we dug up a skeleton. We thought it might be an old Indian burial ground and called in an expert from University of California. He said the bones were those of a woman buried around the turn of the century."

One of the most grisly hauntings ever investigated by Sylvia occurred on Alcatraz Island. "Discovered" in 1775 by Juan Manuel de Ayala, the island of Alcatraz was known by the Miwok Indians as a haven for evil spirits. In 1934 a maximum-security prison was built there, the most hated and feared in the United States penal system. The notorious Al Capone and Machine Gun Kelly were among the hundreds of murderers, robbers, and rapists who ended their days here.

Because of the evil reputation surrounding the place, Alcatraz was finally closed in 1963. Today the stark island lies vacant, a sanctuary for seagulls, but as the prison crumbles, its legend grows.

On September 5, 1984, Rex Norman, a ranger spending a lonely night on the island, was awakened by the sound of a heavy door swinging back and forth in cell block C. Upon investigation, Norman could find nothing to account for the disturbance. When the sounds continued on subsequent nights, it was decided to bring Sylvia in on the case.

On September 10, Sylvia, accompanied by a CBS news team, began her investigation. One of the first areas toured was the prison hospital. As Sylvia was about to enter one of the rooms, she paused in the doorway. "I don't understand this, but I see all kinds of cards and notes all over the walls. They seem to be everywhere."

Norman stepped to her side. "Do you see anything else?"

"The letter *S*. I see an *S*. I don't know what it means."

"Perhaps it stands for Stroud," Norman ventured. "Robert Stroud, the famous 'Birdman,' spent ten and a half years in this room. People think he had birds in his cell but that isn't true. He just studied birds. He had hundreds of notes and cards tacked up all over his cell—things he was learning about birds."

Moving down the hallway, Sylvia entered another room. "Oh, this is awful!" she exclaimed. "I feel such panic, such anguish. It's almost unbearable. There's something else . . . it's cold, it's so terribly cold here."

"This used to be the therapy room," Norman explained. "The most violently psychotic prisoners were brought here to be bathed in ice water and wrapped in icy sheets. It seemed to have a calming effect. Afterwards they would often go to sleep."

As Sylvia progressed to the prison laundry room, she had another strong reaction. "There was violence here. I see a man. He's tall, bald-headed, and he has tiny little eyes. I'm getting the initial *M* but they call him Butcher."

Norman shook his head. "Could be," he said. "I just don't know." Leon Thompson, an ex-convict who'd been invited to join the party, moved forward and stood beside Sylvia. He is an ex-convict who did time on Alcatraz. "I remember a man we used to call Butcher. His name was Malkowitz, Abie Malkowitz, but we called him The Butcher. He'd been a hit man with Murder Incorporated before they caught him. Another prisoner killed him here in the laundry room."

Feeling pity for the spirit of this prisoner who, for some unaccountable reason, chose to remain in the island fortress, Sylvia held a séance in the prison dining room. With Dal's help, she was quickly able to go into a trance. Soon Francine was present.

"What's happening?" Thompson asked. "Do you see him? What's he doing?"

"He's walking toward us. He's standing now on the other side of our table watching us," she explained. Francine spoke now to the spirit. "You don't have to be afraid of us. No one wants to hurt you," she reassured him.

"What does he say?" Dal asked.

"He says, 'I've heard that before.' " Now she addressed the Butcher once again. "When I leave this mortal vehicle I will return to the other side. Come with me, follow me into the light. You will be much happier there. You will find people who will care for you, people who want to help you."

"What does he say?" Dal asked again.

Francine sighed. "He doesn't believe me. He's going to stay here."

And apparently he has, for the rangers who look after the island fortress, now a state park, continue to report eerie disturbances late at night. The prospect of the Butcher's seemingly eternal sentence to the abandoned penal institution continues to prey on Sylvia's mind. She hopes to be allowed to return again to perform yet another séance.

In searching out potential haunts, Sylvia herself might have initially been drawn to Charles Addams–style Victorians with their long, dark corridors, widow's walks, and dramatic staircases. But the ghosts themselves show a profound indifference to such things.

The ghost, it seems, is concerned with *what* happened to him, not where it happened. In most accounts of hauntings, some spirits come back to erase, re-enact, avenge, or simply brood about an awful event or unfulfilled longing. Others, meanwhile, seem inclined to continue in more comfortable earthly patterns.

Judging from the number of individuals reporting spectral contact, one doesn't have to be a professional medium to see a ghost. They attract believers and nonbelievers indiscriminately. What seems to be required is the ability to tune into the electromagnetic field or "vibes." Many may have the ability to do this without even being aware of it.

To be a ghost hunter one needs only a rational outlook, a good memory, a sense of humor, and an inquisitive, flexible mind. Basic equipment begins with a notebook and pencil—tape recorders, thermometers, cameras, and Geiger counters can be acquired as interest increases.

Of all the locations investigated by Sylvia, her favorite remains the haunted toy shop.

Toys "Я" Us in Sunnyvale hasn't yet erected a warning, "Beware of Swooping Teddy Bears," but it may well come to that, for popular local wisdom has it that the place is haunted. It all began in the early summer of 1978 with a talking doll that couldn't. A customer returned the toy to cashier Margie Honey, complaining that it was defective. Margie tilted the doll this way and that, but no sound would come. Satisfied that nothing could be done, she placed the toy in a carton, intending to return it to the manufacturer. No sooner had she closed the lid than the doll began to cry, "Mama! Mama!"

Margie removed the doll, but could elicit no sound. She and the customer both shook it repeatedly, but the cry was still absent. Back into the box it went. The lid was closed and sure enough the crying began again.

"It ceased to be funny," Margie complained to Sylvia. "I called a clerk to take the toy away. It cried all the way to the stockroom."

A few nights later Margie was sitting alone in the employee lounge. Suddenly a large bulletin board secured to the wall began to swing back and forth.

Then, on another evening, Charlie Brown, another employee, and no relation to Sylvia or Dal, was closing up.

He had just locked the door when he heard a banging sound from inside. Brown opened the door, but there was no one there. When he closed and locked the door, the banging began again. The pattern repeated itself several times until Charlie finally gave up and walked away.

Judy Jackson, the store manager, was later confronted by a customer who complained, "There's something strange going on in the women's restroom."

Judy listened in amazement as the woman explained. "I turned off the water faucet," she said, "but by the time I reached the door it had turned itself on again. I went back and turned it off, only to have it turn on again. This happened three times and now it's on again."

One evening, yet another employee carefully stacked a group of skates on a shelf just before closing time. The next morning he returned to find them rearranged in an intricate pattern—on the floor.

None of these phenomena has ever been explained. These and similar cases, some involving merchandise or equipment being moved during the night, are particularly curious. The business is a no-nonsense one and is extremely well organized. The incidents described are entirely out of character.

Employees came to believe that well-secured shelves unaccountably falling, footsteps heard in empty lofts, and lights turning themselves on and off can mean only one thing—a ghost. But of whom—or what?

Ultimately, Margie Honey and another employee, Regina Gibson, decided to mount their own investigation. The search took them to the Sunnyvale Public Library. Among the archives, they found a cryptic note which read, "It is said that the ghost of Martin Murphy is seen on nights of the full moon."

Reputed to be descended from the kings of Ireland, Murphy was the founding father not only of Sunnyvale, but of the surrounding towns of Mountain View and Los

Altos as well. An early pioneer who arrived on the first wagon train to reach California by way of the Sierra Nevada Mountains, Murphy purchased a five-thousand-acre ranch and settled in what would eventually be Sunnyvale.

On July 18, 1881, Martin and Mary Murphy celebrated their golden wedding anniversary with a huge party at their mansion, a great frame building that had been brought from Boston in sections by boat around Cape Horn and reassembled like a great jigsaw puzzle. An estimated ten thousand guests partied there for three days and nights.

Many believed that the Murphy saga didn't end with Martin's death in 1884. Many past and present employees of Toys "Я" Us said that his was a restless spirit still bound to earthly pleasures. They called their resident ghost "Martin." Considering him to be highly mischievous, they speculated about his intentions. Some were frightened.

Martin Murphy named the city streets for his numerous offspring, but his interest in young people extended further; the city father helped to found the University of Santa Clara and the College of Notre Dame in nearby Belmont. So, some speculated, what better vantage point could the ghost of this man—once so fond of children—have found to watch the world go by than a toy store on a corner in the city he had founded?

Sylvia decided to find out for herself. Arranging with the store manager to spend the night at Toys "Я" Us, she and a small research team entered as the last shoppers were ushered out. As always, the staff straightened up the merchandise, putting each toy in place, then swept the floors. Each employee was checked out and the alarm was set. No one could leave or enter before nine the next morning without triggering it.

Despite these precautions, during the night a large bean bag set well back on a shelf tumbled to the floor. Several beach balls belonging on the shelves of Aisle 107 appeared on the floor of Aisle 206. Later that night, a weighted ball was found in the center of a corridor, and put back on its shelf and barricaded in place by a box. Within an hour the ball was back on the floor again—the box pushed to one side.

At midnight, the hour suggested by the television reporters present, Sylvia began her séance, an attempt to psychically "tune in" to the store. To everyone's surprise, she began to describe not Martin Murphy, as most had anticipated, but a circuit preacher whom she "saw" brooding over an unrequited love.

The clergyman's name was John Johnston, though it seemed to her that most called him Yon or Yonny. Sylvia clearly saw him pumping water from a spring that appeared to her bubbling out of a corner of the store. Yonny had stayed with a family who resided on the property, she explained. He fell in love with a pretty girl named Beth, one of the daughters of a prominent family. But she was scarcely aware of his presence and married someone else. Yon or John remained a bachelor. Sylvia saw him limping painfully about the store, blood pouring from an injured leg.

The names Murdock, Josiah Abrams, and Kenneth Harvey also appeared in Sylvia's consciousness. She spoke of tremendous activity within the area now occupied by Toys "Я" Us during the years 1881 and 1923.

The next day a research team from the Nirvana Foundation attempted to validate Sylvia's psychic findings and discovered that a spring, now capped, flowed where the building occupied by Toys "Я" Us now stands. Water was undoubtedly pumped there. But, more important, could Beth possibly have been Martin Murphy's daughter, Elizabeth, who eventually married William Taafee, a prominent citizen of the area? One thing, however, appeared certain. The Murphys—devout Catholics—would scarcely have considered an itinerant Protestant preacher as an appropriate husband for their daughter.

The Murphy wedding anniversary party—an event of such magnitude that court was adjourned for the entire three days to enable judge, jury, prosecutor, and defendant to attend—was held in 1881. The events of 1923 were less easy to pinpoint. Newspaper accounts of the time failed to turn up anything of note—but the team hardly knew what it was searching for. The significant events that Sylvia sensed were probably of a highly personal nature.

Though no connection with Josiah Abrams or Kenneth Harvey was discovered, an attorney named Francis Murdoch was found to have been owner of the *San Jose Weekly Telegraph*. In 1860 Murdoch sold the newspaper to the Murphy family.

The most dramatic find was John Johnston, whose life was recorded in *History of Santa Clara County*. Johnston was a Forty-niner who settled in the Santa Clara Valley. There he became a minister who was instrumental in the founding of the First Presbyterian Church of San Jose. He never married and bled to death in 1884 as the result of an accident sustained while chopping wood.

Prior to the séance, Bill Tidwell, a professional photographer, had placed a camera next to Sylvia. "If you see anything, just pull this string," he'd instructed her. As she saw "Yonny" approach, Sylvia had followed his instructions. When the film was developed, it revealed strange, unexplainable white blobs illuminating the darkened room.

Of course, all the ordinary explanations were considered—faulty equipment, double exposure, light leaks or reflections, faulty development, refractions and, naturally, the imagination of the viewer. Any or all of these could have accounted for the phenomenon, but were ultimately rejected in favor of the spirit itself.

Sylvia was delighted that her information was verified, but couldn't get the thought of John Johnston out of her mind. He seemed such a tragic figure, stuck forever in what must have been a very unhappy situation. Surely there was something that she could do to release him from so sad and unproductive an afterlife.

Another séance was scheduled. Sylvia returned once again to the Toys "Я" Us store where John Johnston maintained his vigil. "It's time for you to move on, John. You've been dead a long time," Sylvia urged.

"No, no," the spirit responded as he shook his head. "I'm waiting for Beth to notice me."

"Beth has been dead a long time, too. If you go to the other side you'll find her. You'll be able to talk to her much more easily there. Everything will be better, I promise."

John shook his head again and began to walk away. He was becoming agitated. "I have to stay here, I have to look after things," he explained, then paused, looking about the large store. "It's different now, there are so many people around. They have so much company now."

"Yes, it must be very different," Sylvia agreed, "lots of children running around."

"Yes, the children are so noisy . . . twin boys running, yelling . . ."

"Twin boys? Did you see them clearly?"

"Oh, yes, I was afraid they would break something. I have to watch things. Beth isn't here. I have to be responsible."

"John, you were a minister—you *are* a minister—you should know there's a heaven. It's waiting for you. Please don't fade out on me. Listen to what I'm saying," Sylvia urged. "Do you see the light? Walk toward it, John."

But John was shaking his head again, already fading away. It was obvious that it disturbed him to hear her speak of death or suggest that he leave his familiar surroundings. Sylvia called out to John, urging him to return, but he did not.

When the lights were turned on again, the store manager

rushed forward. "Of course I could only hear your part of the conversation, but didn't you say something about twin boys?"

"Yes, John was complaining about them. He said that they were very noisy."

"Were they ever! Those kids came in here again today, hell on wheels. Their mother doesn't even attempt to control them, maybe she can't, they're too much for her. They really tear up the place."

Subsequent attempts on Sylvia's part to persuade Johnny to leave Toys "Я" Us and move on to the other side were failures. He has no intention of abandoning his familiar habitat. In John Johnston's confused perspective, his assumed responsibility for looking after the place remains all-important.

"But you must remember that his time and ours are very different," Sylvia gently reminded the toy shop staff. "Some day—maybe next week or perhaps a hundred years from now—the realization will finally come to him that his purpose in this world has been served. Then he'll move easily toward the light and take his place in the spirit world."

The toy shop personnel are now in no hurry to see Johnny go. Convinced at last that their ghost means them no harm, they've adopted him as a kind of pet.

This acceptance of spirit phenomena and willingness to coexist with ghosts is not at all uncommon, Sylvia has found. Perhaps the most persuasive explanation of the continued popularity of the ghostly phenomenon is its implied optimism. A spirit has conquered death and come back to prove it. It is both a clue and an invitation to a world beyond our own limited reality, an offer to broaden our awareness to encompass everything and anything that just might be possible.

And who can resist that kind of challenge?

As a result of Sylvia's many explorations of allegedly

haunted dwellings, a protocol has evolved which she now offers to aspiring ghostbusters.

GHOST-HUNTING PROTOCOL

NO ALCOHOL OR DRUGS BEFORE OR DURING TRANCE

1. The first visit to the location should be the research visit. All people involved should be in attendance; there should be no "test run" by any member of the research party prior to this time.

2. To eliminate the possibility of telepathy, no research on the location should be conducted prior to the research visit.

3. All members of the team should jot down everything they know about the location prior to their arrival.

4. The team should determine before the research visit what it is that they wish to learn about the location while there—what they wish to check for psychically, what they anticipate photographing, and what information they require from the trance control. The purpose of the visit should be determined. Is it to discover if the house is haunted? If so, what material would back up this hypothesis? What questions must be asked of the trance control? What psychic impressions are important? Is the purpose of the visit to determine the history of the house via energy implants? If so, what particular historical eras are important? If there are none, those in attendance should be prepared to ask a variety of questions regarding different historical periods.

5. Researchers should enter the house together and silence should be maintained until the initial walk-through ends. Those participating in the walk-through should record their impressions individually

GHOST-HUNTING PROTOCOL *(continued)*

and without communicating with one another. Since such research often involves the owners or residents of the location under investigation, one team member should be designated as the nonsilent partner who enters the house before the others and makes certain that the group will have immediate access. He or she can also inform the group of any areas which might be designated "off limits." The owner/occupants should be present, but should not give information during the walk-through.

6. After the silent walk-through, the group should meet to discuss their impressions. If necessary, each may return to specific areas for additional sensing. *Before the general discussion of impressions*, all researchers should turn in their notes or tapes to a neutral party (possibly the nonsilent coordinator). Though this may seen an untrusting maneuver, its purpose is to protect team members from being accused of changing their notes to match those of other members.

7. Prior to the trance, the research group should discuss what they wish to know about the location, based on the impressions gathered on the walk-through. Two areas should be foremost: 1) information from the control that either validates or invalidates the impressions gathered, and 2) information that can be verified historically by library/museum/archives research.

8. The trance session should be taped.

9. If only to boost the morale of the research group, the background information on the location should be investigated as soon as possible.

CHAPTER TEN

Mumbi-1

THE two-year-old looked intently and trustingly into Sylvia's eyes. "You died of blood poisoning in your last life," she explained to him. *"You—don't—have—to—die—now. Don't leave us."*

Little David, a leukemia patient, recovered, defying all medical prognostications.

Later, his parents returned to Sylvia, wildly happy but nonetheless puzzled. "How could David understand what you were saying—or did he?" his father asked.

"Kids know much more than most of us realize," Sylvia told him. "They understand what's going on from the very beginning. The next time you look into a new baby's eyes, tell me you don't see, 'Oh, hell, here I am again.' That's what he's *really* thinking. But what we usually say is, 'The baby looks so old and wise.' That's not it at all! He's actually saying, 'Oh, *shit*.' "

"It's that bad, huh?" David's father asked, shaking his head. "I don't understand. What's the point of it all? Why do we do it?"

"Francine says that the purpose of reincarnation is to perfect the soul by gaining different kinds of experience and knowledge in a negative plane of existence—our earth. Perhaps, for whatever reason, it was necessary for you and your child to experience leukemia. That's been accomplished now and you're experiencing something else—a healing. Your boy has literally healed himself just by deciding to do it. Can any of us really be the same after an experience like that?''

"But why do we need to incarnate?" the mother asked. "If it's so bad here in comparison, why can't we just stay on the other side?"

"Well, you can if you want to," Sylvia told him. "At least that's what Francine says, but the thing is, what all of us *really* want is to get better, to *be* better than we are. Some entities choose to work on their perfection on the other side, but the trouble is in their environment, where everything is so perfect, it takes so long. Most entities decide to come back to earth every hundred years or so to have another whack at perfection. There are even a few who elect to spend all their time down here incarnating into one life right after another. I'd call that being gluttons for punishment."

"Then who judges us? Who decides when we've reached perfection?" David's mother persisted.

"We do," Sylvia told her. "We judge ourselves. Doesn't that make sense? We're the ones who know what we need to learn. Francine says that when we're on the other side we're much more understanding of everything. We're fully aware of our good points, too—as well as the bad. We're not confused there. We remember not only everything we learned here in our last past life, but everything we learned in all those other lives. Then, added to that, is all the knowledge we've accumulated while working on the other side."

When David's mother continued to look doubtful, Sylvia reassured her. "No one is going to be standing over your shoulder telling you to work harder, to get better. You're the only one responsible for your learning process. How fast or slow you progress is entirely up to you. There's no good or bad connected with it. It's really more of an evaluation of how you're coming along in your own progression. There's no St. Peter or anyone else to condemn you. If you decide that your accomplishment in a given life isn't at the level you want it to be, you may decide to live another life that's very similar, to see if you can do it better a second time. That's part of the reason reincarnation exists—to give each of us as many chances as we need to learn something, something at which we'd failed. Think of it this way: God's an equal-opportunity employer. Everyone gets all the opportunities that he or she wants to work toward any desired goal.

The man nodded in agreement. "I never believed in reincarnation; I thought it was all nonsense. But listening to you talk to our little boy, and then seeing him actually get well when no one thought it was possible . . . How can we *not* believe that there's something like that going on? But what I don't understand is why he forgot about those other lives, forgot about his blood poisoning, for instance. Why aren't we born with a continuing awareness of our past experiences?"

"Francine says it's so we can learn our lessons the hard way. She believes they have a deeper meaning that way, and are more of an influence on our soul's development."

"But apparently David's past life affected him in *this* life. Is there a way of explaining that?"

"He was very confused, but fortunately I was able to get through to him. A reminder was all he needed. It's unusual to carry a physical ailment over from a past life but it still happens sometimes. Then, such a reminder may help to dispel the new problem. It's a kind of unfinished business, something like the spirits that hang around a so-called 'haunted' house."

Sylvia thought for a moment and then went on. "There's another kind of carryover as well. We bring our likes and dislikes with us. Our personalities have been deeply affected by previous incarnations. Past lives can have a tremendous influence on physical health, appearance, race, creed, religion, value system, wealth, habits, talents, sex—

I could go on and on. There's almost nothing about us that isn't rooted in a past life. Some of what we bring is positive, but some is not—bigotry, for instance. We've all—at some time in some life—been both the perpetrator and the victim of that."

"This whole thing is so new to us, it's kind of overwhelming," David's mother admitted.

"Perhaps you might want to look at your lives and analyze them from the perspective of reincarnation," Sylvia suggested. "See how many of your interests, habits, likes, and dislikes could be the direct result of a past life. Is your house furnished in a particular decor? Do you prefer a specific kind of ethnic food? Do you vacation in the same place year after year because you feel drawn to it? You may be surprised where answers to these questions take you."

The couple left the reading room with lots to talk about. As Sylvia watched them go, she smiled absently, thinking of the many similar conversations she'd had with Francine over the years. The concept of reincarnation had always seemed natural to her but the mechanics were something else. Once, during a particularly low period in her life, she and Francine had discussed suicide. "Couldn't I just leave now and come back another time?" Sylvia had ventured.

"Do you think for an instant that you can simply 'cop out,' as you humans say?" Francine replied. "It is quite impossible. There are no breaks, only your preordained exit points. There is no escaping life. You would only have to face the same problems all over again."

"But I'd be rested, it would be easier," Sylvia reasoned.

"No, it would *not*—it would not be easier," Francine said emphatically. "You would be pushed right back to earth immediately. There would be no rest period allowed. You would be right back in the same geographical location, with the same type of parents, in the same kind of marriage or relationship, with the same work problems, the same financial situation. *Everything* would be the same and you would just have to confront it all over again. Nothing would be gained by trying to escape. Think of it this way. What happens when children run away from school? Don't you put them right back in and keep them there until they graduate? Of course you do, and it isn't until they've learned their lessons and graduate that other opportunities are open to them."

Sylvia remembered, could almost feel her weariness at the time of that conversation, her exhausted frustration. "What will happen to me when I do get to the other side?" she had asked as a child might beg a bedtime story.

"The same thing that happens to everyone. You will move through a dark tunnel toward a shining light where a loved one will be waiting to guide you. At the end of that tunnel you will find an orientation center, our Hall of Wisdom. There you will sit before a screen and watch your whole life pass before your eyes. It is then that you will decide whether or not you have completed the self-assigned tasks of that life. Perhaps you may choose to reincarnate immediately, but more than likely you will choose to pursue your studies on the other side for a time."

"Why would I ever choose to return?" Sylvia had sighed wearily.

"Whatever your decision, you will have help," Francine had assured her. "A counselor will go over your life with you—your blueprint, your life theme, everything. You will decide together what is the best course to follow in order to achieve your own perfection."

"But why did I take on so much this time?" Sylvia had asked. "Why did I make it so hard for myself?"

"That is a tendency of everyone," Francine had admitted. "Life on the other side is so idyllic and one feels so strong that one tends to forget how difficult it is on earth. You are counseled against taking on too much, but once again, the final decision is yours."

"I must have an awfully big mouth."

"Yes, Sylvia," Francine had agreed. "As I told you before, we retain much of our earthly personality on the other side."

"That's a comfort—I guess."

"But it is all your choice," Francine had insisted. "From the beginning of your creation, you, like every other entity, knew what you wanted to perfect, what your life theme would be, and how many lifetimes it would take to achieve perfection. It's that innate knowledge that drives each of us forward. The first one to know when it's time to incarnate is you. It's like a bell going off, an internal clock that says: *'Now.'* "

"Then what happened? How—where—did I go wrong? How did I get into all this?" Sylvia had asked, feeling and sounding petulant.

"You did *not* go wrong," Francine had reassured her. "You are moving according to plan—your very own plan. The first thing you did before incarnating—into this life as well as the previous ones—was review your past history. In the very beginning, in the early days of creation, all entities probed the future of all the planets that were enacting the reincarnation schematic. They studied all periods or ages of the planets—past and future—seeking the one that contained the right scenario for their particular perfection. The evolvement of the planet Earth contained a series of plateaus—the Atlantean era, the Neanderthal period, the Cro-Magnon period, the Stone Age, the Iron Age, the Bronze Age, the Golden Age, the Dark Ages, the Renaissance Age, the Atomic Age. In each of these ages, all entities could find the particular scenario that best fit them."

"Did—do we get whatever we ask for?" There was a trace of eagerness in Sylvia's voice.

"In a sense. In the very early days we all sat in a vast forum scanning all those periods on a great board—a little like a stock market board or a union hiring hall—which apprised us of all available opportunities."

Sylvia had been puzzled. "You mean life opportunities?"

"Yes. The boards listed information like geographical locations, parentage, ethnic and racial backgrounds, politics, economics—everything about a lifetime opportunity down to the most finite detail. Then some of us—you among them—took this information and, knowing our individual needs, bid on various opportunities."

It all seemed very strange to Sylvia. "Bid," she had repeated. "I don't understand."

"In the beginning bidding was necessary because so many entities wanted to incarnate early. They were curious and eager to see what it was like on Earth and there were not enough opportunities for everyone at once. Now, of course, with the population so much larger, there is no longer a problem."

"I'm sure I'd be *glad* to give my place to someone else." Sylvia, thinking of the state of her life, had again been disconsolate.

"No, you were always very eager, very courageous about the tasks you set for yourself. You still are very courageous, Sylvia. You have no idea how much you give of yourself to others or what an inspiration you are."

Sylvia had shaken her head self-deprecatingly. Life had seemed very difficult at that point, getting through each day an effort. Only her responsibility to her children—and in some strange way she couldn't yet define, to Francine—kept her going.

But despite Sylvia's depression, she had been fascinated

by her spirit guide's account. "What happened next?" she had asked.

"You—like everyone else—went to the Council, the governing body for the other side, and submitted a plan for your proposed incarnation. An entity does not *have* to do this, and a few have incarnated without the approval of the Council. But most prefer it and all benefit from the counseling involved. It is like your earthly saying, 'Two heads are better than one.' The expertise and knowledge of the Council Elders combines with your own knowledge to select the best possible incarnation scenario. The Council went over your plan in great detail. They warned you of pitfalls that you had not considered, they pointed out events that might change the whole complexion of what you wanted to accomplish."

"I wish I could remember," Sylvia had sighed wistfully. "Was the Council nice?"

"Oh, yes, very nice. Very loving and caring. They exist for our welfare and well-being. Frequently, a session with the Council causes entities to revise their plans until a final course is reached that takes in all contingency factors. Often an entity is warned about a particular incarnation and is counseled against going into a life that is too difficult or ambitious. Sometimes the Council may advise an entity to take two or three lives to accomplish what has been planned for just one. Of course there are always some entities who will not listen. They argue with the Council, insisting that they are right."

"What does the Council do about that?" Sylvia had wondered.

"Nothing, nothing at all. If the entity refuses to heed their advice, the Council assumes a passive stance. All entities possess free will and can incarnate as they choose. But I can truly say that I have never seen the Council make a mistake in reviewing plans for an incarnation, although I have seen many disastrous mistakes made by an overeager entity."

"Was—is—that the final step?"

"Oh, no. After that, you return to the orientation center, where you discuss the plan that you and the Council have decided upon with at least one Master Teacher. This is a time-consuming process for everyone because the Master Teacher must be totally familiar with every detail of what the entity wants to accomplish. Some entities spend many years of your time—years as you measure time on earth—in the orientation center preparing for life. When you've completed this final preparation, you begin to search with the aid of a computerlike apparatus for the right parents, the right body, the right geographical location. Using this device, you decide upon the defects you might have, the jobs you might hold, what kind of childhood is best for fulfilling your destiny, what kind of midlife, what mate or children, what kind of death."

According to Francine, all these factors are weighed. "You yourself decide whether it would be better for you to be rich or poor," she explained. "Do you want a parent that will be a matriarch or patriarch? Do you want parents who will be divorced or killed? Do you want siblings? Will you marry? What entity or entities will best enable you to attain perfection? Will you have children? How many? What sex? What kind of dispositions should they have? What kind of associations? What kind of traumas? How many negative challenges should you have? Will you embrace one religion, many religions, or no religion? The list of possibilities and necessary decisions goes on and on."

Sylvia had sighed again. "With so much planning, how can it all go wrong?"

"It does *not* go wrong. There is no 'wrong,' " Francine insisted. "Things only seem wrong to you at this time.

Actually, I have not told you all the decision making involved in an incarnation. There is more. After finalizing the basic plan, you and your Master Teacher view the major events of this planned incarnation on an apparatus much like a closed-circuit television. In this manner you actually see the major events and choices in the life that you have planned in order to gauge your reaction and analyze your emotional response. You may look at your prospective life in a hundred different ways—variations made possible by unanticipated changes."

"Then I can make changes in the plan?" Sylvia had asked.

"There are many paths that an entity may follow, but only one 'blue track,' the path that must be followed to accomplish the desired perfection. If the entity gets off this track, some form of derangement may arise."

Sylvia had considered that possibility. "Derangement? What exactly do you mean?"

"Alcoholism could be one type of response, or perhaps some other form of mental or physical illness. In the most extreme cases, it could take the form of suicide. Of course, the entity planning the incarnation is carefully programmed to avoid the stress that produces such problems."

"It doesn't work very well, does it—that programming?" Sylvia had asked.

"Most of the time it *does* work," Francine had argued. "In most cases, the entity survives incarnation, although not always on the chosen track. The difficulty comes, as I have told you before, from the difference between your plane and the other side. Overcoming the problem is the reason for the extensive planning and, particularly, the intensive review. The plan must be programmed into the subconscious mind of the entity so that he or she can not only survive the incarnation but move forward toward perfection."

Sylvia had sat back, thinking about all that Francine had said. "And that's it?" she asked at last.

"Yes, that finally is 'it.' When all the planning, counseling, and programming have been completed and the 'blue track' has been imbedded in the entity's subconscious mind, he or she incarnates."

"And then we're out here floundering around on our own," Sylvia had responded.

"Well, not *really* alone," Francine amended. "We spirit guides are always with you—if only more of you would listen to us."

Though until this time the mechanics of reincarnation had been a mystery to Sylvia, she had been aware of its principles operating in her life since early childhood. When she was scarcely more than a baby she recalled being poisoned in a prior life and so insisted that her father taste all her food before she would eat it. As Sylvia grew older, pleasant memories of convent life contributed to her longing to become a nun in this current incarnation.

Then later still, Dal, shortly after their marriage, hypnotized Sylvia and returned her to an earlier life in Japan. "Are you psychic?" he asked.

"Yes," she replied. Then, while still under the hypnotic trance, Sylvia startled her husband by asking, "Are you one of my voices?" It was an insightful moment that seemingly transcended time and space. For an instant two lifetimes separated by hundreds of years had merged into one.

This was a tragic life, one that Sylvia chose not to focus on for long. Her ability to hear voices that others did not hear, to see things psychically that others could not see, was highly threatening to those around her. At first her words were dismissed as the ravings of a madwoman, but eventually a woman frightened by a prediction about herself stabbed the entity who was Sylvia in that incarnation. She died of those wounds.

Sylvia believes today that it was necessary for her to experience that negative potential of a psychic's life to fully comprehend the power inherent in this gift.

Later, an indication of a chain of lives influenced by psychic ability in Sylvia's past surfaced when another regression revealed a life as an oracle in Delphi. As usual, Dal had relaxed her, leading Sylvia deeper and deeper into a hypnotic trance. "Now open your eyes," he instructed her at last. "Look about you . . . what do you see?"

"Mountains, steep jagged mountains . . . they're all around me."

"What are you doing?"

"I'm climbing a trail. It's very steep and rocky."

"Are you a man or a woman?"

"I'm a woman."

"What are you wearing? First look at your feet. What kind of shoes are you wearing?"

"Sandals. I'm wearing sandals. Sandals and a long white gown, a kind of tunic."

"Are you alone?"

"No, there's a little girl with me. She's dressed as I am. I'm holding her hand. She's my daughter."

"Are you happy?"

"No, it's early morning, but I feel so tired, so very tired. At the top of the trail there are a group of cell-like rooms. I will go into one of them. I do this every day. Soon long lines of people will be climbing this trail to see me, to ask me questions."

"Do you foretell the future for them?"

"Yes, I do that every day from early morning until late at night. My little daughter is training to do it too."

"Don't you like your life?"

"I have no life—no life of my own. All my time is spent reading for others. I see very little of my child."

"What about her father?"

"He's gone . . . long ago . . . I can't seem to remember. I'm very much alone in this life. It's all work, all readings. I have very little contact with anyone. The people who come to me stand at a little window in my cell. I'm busy all the time, but it's really very lonely."

"How do you die?"

"Tuberculosis. I'm not sorry. It feels so heavy, not just my chest, but everything. I am ready to move on."

After returning to consciousness, Sylvia had total recall of this past incarnation. After meditating on it, she came to the conclusion that the memory was meant to instill in her an awareness of the necessity of balance in a medium's life.

In 1983, while vacationing in Greece, Sylvia became ill and was unable to accompany Dal on an eagerly antici- pated excursion to Delphi. At her urging, he made the trip alone. On Dal's return to Athens that evening, he started to describe the mountain sanctuary to her. "Wait a minute," Sylvia said, stopping him, "you forget—I've been there, too." And then she went on to describe for him the steep trails, the towering peaks, massive columns and statuary.

Yet for all her experiences—not only from her own past life memories, but from helping others to recapture theirs—Sylvia was unprepared for the wave of nostalgia that assailed her in 1981 as she stepped off the plane in Nairobi, Kenya. The trip had been largely unplanned. Client friends who had moved to Africa had invited Sylvia and Dal to visit them there. The Browns had accepted, but frantic schedules had kept them too busy to read or even to think much about the country in advance of the trip. Sylvia knew almost nothing about Africa, at least not consciously. Yet as her feet touched African soil, she felt an immediate sense of coming home. As time passed, pictures and incidents appeared in her mind's eye. Sylvia is certain that she has lived three very happy lives in Kenya.

In the first of these, she saw herself dressed in the red wraparound robes of the Massai tribe. Sylvia's husband in that incarnation was killed on a hunting expedition, but her son—who is Chris in *this* lifetime—cared for her in a loving and tender way throughout her long life. In another incarnation, this one as a member of the Kikukyu tribe, it was Sylvia who was killed by a wild animal. She recalls this incarnation today as a short, almost idyllic life. In each of her African existences, Sylvia was both a woman and a shaman. She remembers this as a very natural thing that was well integrated into her simple life and taken for granted by those around her. Only in the final incarnation, that of a Samburu, did she achieve any kind of prominence. This occurred when she was able to effect a dramatic healing of a village child, but even this was a low-keyed experience that had little effect upon the simple rhythms of her life.

Sylvia believes that the purpose of these lives was to learn the value of simplicity and of a natural, uncomplicated existence. These lives also helped her to reach an understanding of a loving cooperation with others. Each of her African incarnations was dedicated to these principles and a return to the areas served as a reminder of truths she'd always known but tended at times to forget.

It appears that there still remains a part for Sylvia to play in Africa. During the course of her holiday, she was interviewed by a local journalist, Kathy Eldon. Eldon had approached the assignment with some trepidation. She'd never met a psychic before and wasn't at all certain that she wanted to. Later she was to write, "I went cautiously, determined to wipe from my brain any transparent thoughts which could be 'picked up' and used to reveal me. But Sylvia in person held no terror. She's a big, comfortable lady with tinted blonde hair, huge eyes outlined in blue eye shadow, and a voice which is deep and husky."

In the interview Sylvia talked intimately about her experiences, beginning with precognition in early childhood. She described the entrance of Francine into her life and outlined the scope of the Nirvana Foundation. "Suddenly," Eldon recalls, "in the middle of our conversation, Sylvia began talking about me. She told me how many children I have, their sexes, and gave accurate descriptions of their personalities.

"She discussed a trip I would be making, which I had planned only the day before. She talked about a book I would be writing and discussed medical complaints I had experienced in the past. She used words to describe me that only my best friend would have chosen, and pinpointed an incident two years back which led to my present job. I was astounded. Sylvia had no way of doing research on my life, and indeed, much of the information she imparted was known only to me."

Her earlier concerns completely banished, Eldon took Sylvia to meet Mark Horton, an Oxford don who had excavated ancient ruins off the coast of Mombasa. Sylvia was able to successfully date coins which he showed to her and to identify where they had been found on a map of Kenya. Then she went on to point out to him a place where other significant artifacts could be found.

The journalist then introduced Sylvia to a most skeptical gentleman, Dr. Richard Wilding, the National Museum's Director of Coastal Sites and Monuments. After commiserating with Wilding about a hip ailment that he'd had from birth but which was not visible to anyone else, Sylvia set off with Wilding and Eldon for Gedi, a deserted city mysteriously vacated in the fifteenth century. After walking about the site for a few minutes, Sylvia began to sense the vibrations of the people who'd lived there. "This area drew a lot of children," Sylvia told Wilding, pointing to a mound of old stones. "Children of all ages came here with their parents."

Wilding looked at her in amazement. "We believe these to be the ruins of a family mosque," he told her. "Do you have any feelings as to why the city was deserted? Why did they all leave?"

"People died here . . . a lot of them all at once. It was the water. Something polluted the water system and most of them died. The rest moved away and never came back."

"Yes! yes!" he exclaimed, nodding, his earlier skepticism gone, "that could account for the exodus very well indeed."

The article that Eldon wrote about Sylvia for her newspaper, *The Nation*, touched a sensitive spot in many readers. Within a week, the journalist had received more than fifty letters and calls from people anxious to make contact with Sylvia, who by then had, unfortunately, returned home. Undaunted, two of these readers went on to telephone Sylvia in California for readings.

One woman, distraught by the disappearance of a teenage son, asked for information on his whereabouts. "Is he alive?" she wanted to know. "Is he being held under duress? How can we get him back?"

Sylvia's response was instant. Describing the events which had led to the boy's disappearance, she gave details about the people he was with, described where he was staying, and added, "Don't bother to look for him. You won't find him. He'll come home when he is ready." The family relayed the information to the police, who continued their search. Despite their efforts to follow up clues furnished by the boy's friends, the youngster wasn't found.

Then on Easter Sunday, the runaway boy came home—just as Sylvia had said he would. He later confirmed most of the information in Sylvia's prediction.

The second call to the United States was made by a Tanzanian reader of *The Nation*, who was so distressed by his wife's mysterious illness that he felt that it was essential that he discuss her case with Sylvia.

But once again there was no need for details. "Your wife has severe headaches which constrict her circulation," Sylvia told him. After relating more information on the woman's condition, which the husband corroborated, she recommended a specific medicine.

The patient, who had for months consulted many doctors in her country, decided to try the new medicine. After one week, instead of being bedridden with incapacitating headaches every day, she reported only two mild headaches in six days. She appeared, on the basis of her conversation with Kathy Eldon, to be well on the road to recovery.

The article that Eldon had written for *The Nation* appeared in February 1982. At that time Sylvia warned that there would be serious difficulties in Kenya during the end of July or the beginning of August. On the first of August a coup attempt resulted in several deaths and a shakeup of the government.

The following year, when Sylvia returned, she was contacted by cabinet member Phillip Leakey, son of the world-famous anthropologists. During the course of the reading, Sylvia expressed concern about the safety of Kenya's president, Daniel Moi. "He should be very careful in Mombasa . . . I see him there surrounded by flags. He shouldn't be there. It's in September. He's in a kind of—well at home we'd call it a fairground. Someone there wants to hurt him . . . he shouldn't go," she warned.

As it turned out, President Moi's executive duties did take him to Mombasa, where he attended an annual festival, very much like a large state fair. The atmosphere was very tense. Aware of Sylvia's warning, Moi ordered extra security and—most importantly—cut his visit short, possibly averting violence and death.

Today Sylvia is known in Kenya by the Kikukyu title,

"Mumbi-1," which means "First Woman of the World." She has made five trips since 1981 and considers Kenya a second home.

Sylvia has been told by Francine that she's had fifty-four lives. She recalls fragments of twelve but has no particular interest in further pursuing her own past history. These memories have come to her, she believes, for a specific purpose that has some bearing on *this* life. They are long-ago memories from long-distant times. More recent experiences have eluded her. Unless some occasion should arise in which past lives have immediate effects upon this present one, Sylvia remains content to leave them buried.

Once satisfied as to the continuity of the human spirit, mere curiosity isn't enough to justify to her the time spent on hypnotic regression. She prefers to spend the time and energy helping others to heal themselves through knowledge of past-life experiences.

A dramatic demonstration of this was documented on television on October 9, 1982. The subject was Edwinna Moore, hostess of the San Francisco TV show, *Pacific Currents*. Moore's problem was a fear of heights that was severely restricting her life.

Sylvia began by calming her subject, instructing Moore to feel the relaxation creeping slowly over her entire body, beginning with her feet and moving upward. "With each breath, you're going to go deeper and deeper," Sylvia intoned. "Now close your eyes and look at the bridge of your nose." Within a few minutes, Moore was in a deep hypnotic trance.

"Now go to the time when your fear of heights began," Sylvia directed. "Tell me what's happening."

"I'm climbing a mountain," Moore said, her voice almost a whisper. "I'm afraid, I'm so afraid."

"Go back before that time . . . tell me about yourself. What do you look like?"

"I'm young, about fifteen. I have brown skin."

"Where are you?"

"On an island, a very lush island . . . it's Hawaii."

"What's happening?"

"I'm running . . . I'm running away from someone, but it's hard, the mountain's so steep . . . something terrible is going to happen!"

"Who are you running from? Why are you afraid?"

"A woman is chasing me. She's very angry . . . she wants to kill me."

"Why is this happening?"

"Her husband—he fell in love with me. She hates me. I'm to blame."

"What's happening now?"

"I've reached a rope bridge . . . I'm running across a deep chasm. If I can get across I'll be safe . . . the rope is swinging—it's hard to hold on. There are rocks below . . . Oh, she's on the bridge, too. . . . She's reaching out. I can't get away from her . . . I'm holding onto the rope railing but she's making the bridge swing. It's terrible I can't hold on any longer. I'm falling! Oh, I'm falling—"

"It's all right," Sylvia soothed her. "That's all over now. You don't have to experience it. This is a new life that has nothing to do with the other one. You don't have to be afraid of heights any longer. You know now what caused that fear and it's all over. This is a whole new life and you're completely free. I'm going to count to three now and then you'll awaken feeling well and rested. The fear of heights will be gone. One . . . two . . . three . . . Wake up!"

Edwinna Moore did indeed awaken feeling well and rested. Four months later, on February 10, 1983, she wrote to Sylvia,

I wanted to let you know that since our session my fear of heights has virtually disappeared. I'm now able to drive Highway 1 without that shaky feeling in my legs. I can even stand on the edge of a cliff and not feel dizzy. Thank you for releasing me from that debilitating problem.

Not every client has been immediately accepting of the principle of reincarnation. One woman complained to Sylvia about sudden behavior problems that had developed with her four-year-old daughter. They had recently moved into a new apartment with no bathtub. When the child was confronted with a shower she began to scream.

"Poor thing," Sylvia sympathized, "but can you blame her? She was killed in a Nazi gas chamber. The last thing she recalls is being led to the 'showers.' You'll have to explain it to her. She doesn't understand that this is a new life."

The client was shocked. "You can't know something like that!" she argued.

"Why not?" Sylvia countered. "It's no different from telling you what your new place looks like when I haven't been there."

The woman was unconvinced. "It's different to me! I don't believe in reincarnation." She dismissed the idea as absurd, but the following day she called back. The previous night she'd been about to step into the shower when the little girl began to shriek, "No, Mommy, no! Gas!"

The tragic reaction was too much for the mother to deny. "You must be right," she admitted to Sylvia, "but what does it mean? Why would my little girl choose such a terrible life? And what about Hitler and the other Nazis? Why do these awful things happen?"

"I used to wonder about it, too," Sylvia told her. "I'm partly Jewish and so, of course, I've thought a lot about Hitler and the Nazis. Francine says there are actually group incarnations. In the case of the Holocaust, both the persecutors and their victims agreed prior to their lives on earth to enact those horrors."

"But why? What purpose could it serve?"

"It was intended as a global lesson for all of mankind. The same kind of thing happened nearly two thousand years ago in Rome. Both Christians and Romans incarnated together to enact that grim—but inspiring—scenario."

"Then you actually believe that Hitler chose to be Hitler?"

"Yes, I certainly do," Sylvia assured her. "What he did—his acts—was undeniably terrible; but we can never judge an individual. Francine is always reminding me that we all choose lives to express many things. But the ultimate reason is the evolvement of our souls and, finally, of mankind. Some of us select lives in which we are pawns, thereby enabling others to attain perfection in some way. Perhaps the entity who is now your little girl was one of these pawns in her last life."

"I just don't understand that at all," the mother protested.

"We sometimes incarnate to create a certain situation or environment for someone else," Sylvia explained. "On our plane every victim must have a victimizer, every follower a leader. We're all here to help each other. All of us want to end the reincarnation chain so that none of us must live any longer than necessary with negativity."

"But the Holocaust was so terrible, so uniquely terrible—"

"Terrible surely, but not as unique as you might imagine. Many more were killed by the Inquisition, which lasted for a much longer period—more than five hundred years—and encompassed all of Europe as well as Mexico and Central and South America. We tend to think that everything that touches us is unique. We're always saying,

'I wonder if anyone thinks as I do?' You can be certain that somebody does, has, or will. No thought comes into your head that's new. Someone, some place has already had that same thought. In the very early days, new situations on earth were in great demand by incarnating entities, but now there's really nothing new. You may imagine that you're going through a unique situation, but be assured that someone has already experienced it. We are all brothers and sisters in experience."

"But when will it end?"

"It will end when all people have acquired the amount of knowledge necessary for their perfection, when all of us have been sufficiently exposed to negativity and learned all that we can from it."

"Then in other words, you're saying that Hitler was simply a volunteer or possibly an actor playing a part?"

"That's right," Sylvia said as she nodded. "As evil as the acts are that he committed, the entity was a kind of actor playing a villain in a cosmic drama."

"But what about all that karma stuff that people are always talking about? It seems like Hitler would have terrible karma."

Sylvia sighed in exasperation. "I'm so sick of that word. It seems as though just when we finally moved away from the fear of hell, some jackass had to substitute karma."

Deeply puzzled, the woman asked, "Well, just what is karma?"

"The true definition of karma is simply experience," Sylvia told her. "It's nothing more than the experience we seek while incarnated on earth. Unfortunately, many people interpret it in a very negative sense. They think if I slap you in this life, you have to slap me next time and then I slap you back and we just go on slapping each other back and forth through all eternity. Isn't that dumb? As though we didn't have enough to do."

"But if that isn't true, where does the negative connotation come from?"

Sylvia explained, "It began in Eastern philosophy, in which it is believed that 'bad' actions incur bad karma. Some are so extreme that if you were having an accident of some kind, a believer might refuse to help for fear of interfering with your karma. In our own society, the belief in a vengeful, wrathful God sometimes carries over into reincarnation, bringing a false interpretation of negativity to karma. What both of these factions fail to realize is that the whole purpose of life is for people to help one another. It's only in that way that we all progress toward perfection."

"It's hard for me to even think of things like Hitler and the Holocaust, much less imagine volunteering for them," the woman admitted. "But I do wonder about my daughter and myself. We're so close. Do you think perhaps we made some kind of contract before our incarnations to be together?"

"Very probably," Sylvia told her. "Francine says that each single incarnation is part of a highly sophisticated network of other incarnations—your own as well as those of others. Most are planned years in advance so that all the entities involved are subconsciously aware of all the major influences involved. Probably you and your daughter chose each other before you even incarnated. Perhaps you got together on the other side and went over your plans together. Very likely you may have done this with your husband as well and possibly with your parents.

"Of course," she continued, "there are other cases where less time is devoted to planning, but the entities participating still know basically what to expect, even though they might not have conferred with one another. For example, an entity may incarnate without really knowing what soul will incarnate as her child. All she knows is how that 'child' will fit into her overall plan. This method is used less frequently, but is not unusual."

"Then making contracts is all part of the reincarnation process?"

"Oh, very definitely," Sylvia told her, "but the most significant contract is made with your spirit guide or guides."

"How does that work?"

"Francine says that while we're on the other side we usually choose a friend or someone we respect and have confidence in to become our spirit guide when we incarnate. This is a very serious and significant choice, for the spirit guide must know all our plans for incarnation in order to enable us to accomplish as much as possible. If for some reason we get off the track, our guides try to put us back. These leaders observe all our actions in life and help us to evaluate them after passing over to the other side. The devotion and effort of spirit guides are happily given, for they too have used the services of a guide at some point—everyone does—and they wish to help others as they have been helped. After all, this is how we all progress."

"Then how do we get it together? How do we get here?"

Sylvia was pleased with the insight the woman's questions demonstrated. "Remember, I don't recall any of this either," she reminded her. "I used to be as confused as you are. I'm only telling you what I've learned from Francine, but it appears that we enter a kind of tunnel—it's the same one that we leave by when our physical life is over. The tunnel connects the earth plane and the other side. It's here somewhere that our conscious memory starts to fade. Many of us try to hold onto it, but it's never any use. Since thoughts are still things in the tunnel—as they are on the other side—we can think our way to the vehicle that we've chosen. We enter this vehicle—our mothers—

by way of her pituitary gland and then move into the womb. The whole process takes a little over two minutes. Sometimes she's aware when this happens, but most often not."

"Does this happen at conception?"

"No, somewhere between four and eight months into pregnancy. Sometimes at this point an entity, for any number of reasons, will change his or her mind. That's why there are so many miscarriages. It also explains many crib deaths and the high infant mortality rate in third-world countries as well. An entity can return to the other side at will until age four and does so if the soul finds it can't acclimatize to the negativity of Earth. If we thought it was tough on us having kids, it was even tougher on them getting here. The exit from the womb is very traumatic— those bright lights, rough hands, the cold heavy atmosphere and that tiny little body. Francine says it's terribly hard for arriving souls to adapt, but unfortunately the birth process is the only way to incarnate. The birth experience really drives home in a hurry the fact that life on Earth is full of truly negative experience."

As a striking demonstration of soul survival, reincarnation has a particular fascination for Sylvia. She's been actively involved in reincarnation research almost from the inception of the Nirvana Foundation, and today has some seventeen hundred histories on file. Never has a subject failed to remember some detail, however minor, of a past life—and most often this has been related to some problem in this incarnation.

All regressions at Nirvana are tape-recorded so that the individual will have a permanent record of all that transpired, as well as a copy for research purposes. Imagination, patience, and just plain luck are essential to anyone seeking to investigate his or her prior existence. Not everyone has led a recent past life, or even a life within the last

several hundred years. Some of Sylvia's clients have recalled lives spent on other planets. One woman described
a life as a computer operator on Uranus.

In the beginning, Sylvia made an effort to document the
memories uncovered through her numerous regressions
with startling success. One example was a woman who not
only recalled her name in a past life—Selena Franklin—
but her city of residence—Peoria, Illinois. Selena recalled
her husband's name, Edward, and said that they'd both
been born in 1804 and had lived all their lives in Peoria.
A member of the foundation traveling to Peoria was able
to actually locate both graves in a local cemetery and to
verify several other details provided by Sylvia's regression.

For a time Sylvia was very excited by such validations
and worked extensively with the Federal Archives and
Records Center in San Bruno, California, but now feels
that the healing potential of regression offers much more
real satisfaction. Not only are many of the lives recalled
too ancient to document, but the time involved in this type
of research appears wasted when compared to the benefits
of the healings themselves. Is it really worth the effort to
attempt to locate the grave of the teenage temptress who
was Edwinna Moore in a previous incarnation when simply
determining the cause of her death in that life will cure
the fear that had virtually paralyzed the entity in *this*
incarnation?

One unique conclusion that Sylvia has drawn from her
numerous hypnotic regressions is that all entities not only
choose to perfect themselves but they also select a major
life theme with which to achieve that perfection. Sometimes there are two or three subthemes as well. Lately
Sylvia has begun to compare this concept to the choice of
a major and a minor in college.

Each entity, Sylvia believes, carries that main theme
through all its incarnations into a variety of environments
and lifestyles. As each entity has a choice of theme, each

also decides upon the degree of knowledge it wishes to acquire on that theme. Again, comparisons can be drawn to education. While some people might be quite satisfied to graduate from high school, others would be comfortable with nothing less than a Ph.D.

As Sylvia's research continued, she was astonished by the number and variation of themes. "Just how many are there, anyway?" she at last asked Francine. She was even more astonished when Francine responded that there are forty-five.

Soon it became obvious to Sylvia that when individuals lost sight of their themes—their inner missions—they became anxious or even ill. Slowly she began to categorize the themes and to study how each manifested itself in its particular entity. Wasn't this the very key to the question plaguing nearly everyone: *Why am I here?*

Sylvia suggests meditation after a careful reading of the list. Everyone will certainly be able to identify their personal theme, and its recognition may contribute significantly to maintenance and restoration of order in their lives.

LIFE THEMES

Activator—The focus here is to perform tasks that others have failed to accomplish. These may be truly gargantuan or quite menial, but the focus is always on getting the job done right. Activators are the turn-around artists or the trouble-shooters of the world, the ones who successfully reverse failure. Naturally, these entities are in great demand and so have a tendency to spread themselves too thin. Activators should make every effort to confine their energies to tasks where a genuine opportunity to achieve beneficial change exists.

Aesthetic Pursuits—Music, drama, crafts, painting, and writing are included in this category. An aesthetic theme is not to be confused with a little "flair" for one of those enterprises. When an aesthetic theme is present the entity is driven by his or her innate talent. A need to create manifests itself at a young age and dominates the individual's entire life. If the secondary theme is a complementary one, the entity has a long and productive career. If not, the acclaim and privilege the entity receives only lead to dissipation and often tragedy. The life of Richard Burton is a recent example of this. The agonized existence of Vincent van Gogh reflects a very different but equally tragic application of a conflicting secondary theme.

Analyzer—Not only does this entity want to know everything, but how it works and why. Analyzers are afraid they will miss something or that some detail will be overlooked. The rest of us learn from their continuing scrutiny of the most minute detail. These entities thrive in scientific or highly technical settings, where their skills are essential. In everyday life situations the challenge is to let go and trust the senses. Analyzers should, after a discreet analysis of the behavior of others, ask the Holy Spirit for enlightenment to transcend the physical evidence.

Banner Carrier—The first lieutenant of the cause fighter may be found picketing, demonstrating, or possibly lobbying; these entities also fight the battle against injustice. The key to success in achieving this theme is moderation, tact, and discrimination. It is far better for these entities to select one cause and see it through than to scatter their impact among many.

Builder—These entities are the cornerstones of society, the unsung heroes and heroines of wars and organizations. Good parents are often builders, enabling their children to go on to a much larger canvas. Gorbachev is an uncharacteristically visible example of this life theme in action. Without these cogs, the wheels would never turn, yet builders rarely receive credit for the accomplishments made possible by their efforts. They need to keep in mind that not all prizes are won on this plane of existence. Often those who get the credit on earth are not perfecting as rapidly as the builders who help to make their accomplishments possible.

Catalyst—Here are the thinkers and innovators, those agents of action who make things happen. Catalysts are the classroom stars whom everyone aspires to be, the ones invited to parties to ensure excitement. Catalysts—Ralph Nader is a prime example here—are essential to society for their innovations. Catalysts generally have boundless energy and actually appear to thrive on stress. They must have an arena in which to perform or they become morose and counterproductive.

Cause Fighter—The number of causes is infinite—peace, whales, hunger, and so on—and the cause fighter will either be drawn to them or will create more. These entities fulfill an important function by speaking for others who are perhaps too absorbed with their own themes to address social issues. Cause fighters have a tendency toward impulsiveness that can place themselves *and others* in jeopardy. It is also essential that cause fighters consider the possibility that the cause itself is minimal compared to their ego involvement.

Controller—The challenge for this entity is obvious. Napoleon and Hitler were typical examples of this theme manifested in its most negative sense. The controller feels compelled to not only run the broad overall show but to dictate to others how they must perform the smallest detail of their lives. In order to perfect, these entities must learn self-control.

Emotionality—Not only the highs and lows but every subtle nuance of emotion will be felt by these entities. Frequently, emotionality is a secondary theme of poets and artists. As such, it will indeed enhance creativity while imposing a severe challenge. The recognition of a need for balance is all-essential here, as is the establishment of self-control.

Experiencer—It's not unusual for this entity to go from flower child to bank president to vagabond touring the world in a self-made boat. Experiencers dabble in nearly everything and master many of their pursuits. Howard Hughes is a well-known example. Wealth is merely a by-product of a multifaceted experience. Good health is essential to an experiencer; it is important not to jeopardize this by excesses.

Fallibility—These entities appear to be always at the wrong place at the wrong time, for they have entered life with a physical, mental, or emotional handicap. Helen Keller, who as an infant contracted a fever that left her deaf and blind, is an excellent example. Her triumph over these handicaps is an inspiration to everyone. It is important for entities with a fallibility theme to remember that they chose this path in order to set an example for the rest of us.

Follower—Initially, these entities might have preferred to be leaders, but on some level they decided not to make the necessary commitment. The challenge of the follower is to realize that leadership is impossible without them and so recognize their own importance. Perfection comes from accepting the self-chosen theme and providing the leader with the best support possible. Discrimination is essential here in deciding exactly who and what to follow.

Harmony—Balance remains all-important to these entities, and they will go to any length to maintain it. Their personal sacrifices are admirable up to a point, but the real challenge lies in the acceptance of life's wrinkles. What can't be changed must be adapted and accepted.

Healer—Entities with this theme are naturally drawn to some aspect of the healing professions, physical or mental. The good they do is obvious. The only danger is that they can easily become too empathetic. It is essential that those with a healer theme pace themselves so that they avoid burnout.

Humanitarian—While cause fighters and banner carriers cry out against the wrongs committed by and against mankind, the humanitarian theme takes these entities into the action itself. Humanitarians are too busy bandaging, teaching, holding, building, and so on, to have time for protests. Those in this category aren't much concerned with the concept of evil and they are inclined to excuse mankind for its faults. Since humanitarians rarely stop with family and friends, reaching far beyond to anyone and everyone who touches them, they are in danger of over-extending themselves. The challenge for the humanitarian—Sylvia Brown's challenge—is to avoid physical burnout through self-love and nourishment.

Infallibility—These entities are born rich, handsome, attractive, witty, and so forth. When we consider that perfection is the universal goal, this theme becomes one of the most challenging. There is often a tendency toward excesses of all kinds. It is almost as though the entity wants to tempt fate. Curiously, there may often be a lack of self-esteem that causes the entity to fear that he or she is not lovable as an individual. The goal here is to truly accept the theme and learn to live with it.

Intellectuality—Here is the theme of the professional student. Charles Darwin, who used the knowledge that he acquired through intensive study to experiment, hypothesize, and eventually publish, is an excellent example of one who has perfected this theme. But since knowledge for its own sake is frequently the goal among intellectuals, there is often a danger that the knowledge that has been so ardently sought and painfully acquired will go nowhere.

Irritant—Deliberate fault finders, entities with the theme of irritant are essential to the perfection of others for, in their company, we are forced to learn patience and tolerance. Though it's important not to play into the irritant's innate pessimism, we must also be nonjudgmental. We must remember that irritants are perfecting their themes so that we can perfect ours through them.

Justice—Many of our founding fathers, concerned as they were with fairness and equality, are examples of the justice theme in operation. Those with justice as a theme will eagerly give their names when they've witnessed an accident or crime. As admirable as all this sounds, it is essential that these entities use discretion in their choices. Mob violence is another misguided attempt to right a wrong. It is imperative that those with justice as a theme remain God-centered.

Lawfulness—Practicing or teaching law are obvious choices for these entities, who are almost obsessed by issues of legality. Some of those entities may also be found serving on governing boards. When elevated, these souls keep the world safe and balanced, but they must always be on guard against the possibility of using their power in a self-serving manner.

Leader—Those who pursue this theme are controlled and premeditated—rarely innovative. They become leaders in areas that are already established. Their drive is toward success rather than creation. Their challenge is to avoid power trips.

Loner—Though often in the vanguard of society, those with the theme of loner invariably pick occupations or situations in which they are in some way isolated. Sylvia, as an example, has recognized this as a secondary theme of her own. Being a psychic has set her apart from others. Loners are generally happy with themselves but should watch their irritation levels when people come into their space. If each theme recognizes the presence and significance of other themes, the result will be far greater tolerance and understanding in the world and—eventually—peace.

Loser—Entities with a loser theme are extremely negative, though unlike those with fallibility as a theme, they are born without handicaps. Often they have many good points, but choose to ignore them. Though their theme may resemble that of the irritant in the proclivity for constant criticism, they are different in that they invariably place the blame back on "poor me." These entities are prime martyrs, moving from one elaborate soap opera to another. By observing this theme in action, we determine to be more positive. It is important that we not judge the people who have this theme, remembering that their patterns were chosen to enable us to perfect ourselves.

Manipulator—This is one of the most powerful themes, for manipulators are easily able to control situations as well as people. By viewing people and situations as a chessboard, those with a manipulator theme can move people and circumstance to their advantage, as though they were pawns. President Franklin Roosevelt was a prime example of a manipulator in action. When such a person works for the good of others, this theme is elevated to its highest purpose. When the theme is misused, the ultimate goal of perfection takes a long time to achieve.

Passivity—Surprisingly, entities with a passivity theme are actually active—but about nothing. Though they will at times take stands on issues, it is always in a nonviolent manner. Although any extreme is hurtful to the individual, *some* tension may be needed in order to bring about the perfection of the soul.

Patience—The patience theme is clearly one of the most difficult paths to perfection. Those with this theme seem to desire a more rapid attainment of perfection than entities with less challenging themes. Often, they carry great amounts of guilt when they feel that they have strayed from their goal and become impatient. This attitude can lead to self-abasement and, sometimes, to suppressed anger. These entities must be lenient with themselves, for living through the circumstances they have chosen to express this theme is difficult enough.

Pawn—The biblical Judas was the classic example of this theme. Whether the means is negative or positive, pawns trigger something of great magnitude into being. We cannot evolve toward universal perfection without the pawn, but those entities who select this theme should preserve their dignity by only picking worthy causes.

Peacemaker—Entities who select the theme of peacemaker are not as pacific as the name implies. Peacemakers are actually pushy in their desire for and pursuit of peace. They work endlessly to stop violence and war addressing a larger audience than those who've opted for harmony as a theme. Their goal of peace far exceeds an allegiance to one particular group or country.

Performance—Those with a performance theme find it highly rewarding but frequently exhausting. These entities are the true "party animals." Some will go into actual entertainment careers, but others will simply be content to entertain in their homes or offices. The challenge here is for those with performance as a theme to combat burn-out by looking within, thus acquiring the ability to nourish and "entertain" themselves.

Persecution—This arduous theme is chosen to allow others to grow spiritually. Entities with a persecution theme live their lives in anticipation of the worst, certain that they are being singled out for persecution. Experiencing pleasure can throw them into a panic because they are convinced that somehow they must pay for it.

Persecutor—Those with a persecutor theme may range from wife beaters and child abusers to mass murderers. It's difficult to see the purpose of this theme within a single lifespan, but these seeming "bad seeds" have a self-chosen role to play that enables mankind to evolve toward perfection. Once again, it is imperative that we not attempt to judge the individual.

Poverty—The theme of poverty appears most frequently in third-world countries, yet it can be even more of a challenge in affluent societies. Some entities with poverty as a theme may even have all they need to be comfortable and yet *feel* poor. With progress, the frenzy fades and is slowly replaced by a sense of bliss as the realization comes that the trappings of this world are transitory things whose importance will quickly pass.

Psychic—The theme of psychic is more a challenge than a gift, at least in the early stages. An entity with this theme is able to hear, see, or sense things in a manner beyond that of natural sense perception. Often it comes to those in strict backgrounds where authority figures strive to deny or suppress the gift. Eventually, the entity will learn to accept and live with the ability, using it for good in a spiritual, if not professional, manner. Sylvia, incidentally, does not carry this theme; psychic ability has never been a challenge point in her life.

Rejection—This challenging theme manifests itself early, with rejection or alienation experienced in childhood. The syndrome accelerates with entry into school and subsequent involvement in relationships. Often these entities are deserted by those they love—even their own children will adopt surrogate mother or father figures. The pattern can be broken once the entity recognizes what is happening and surrenders the action and the ego involvement to God.

Rescuer—One often finds the rescuer working alongside the cause fighter, but when the cause fighter moves on to another cause, the rescuer remains to care for the victim. Even when the victims have obviously created their own problems, the rescuer is determined to "save" them. Often, in so doing, it is the rescuer who is victimized. An entity with a rescuer theme has a high degree of empathy and can manifest strength for those in need. This theme presents a tough road to travel, but the spiritual rewards are great indeed.

Responsibility—Individuals who have chosen the responsibility theme embrace it with fervor rather than obligation and feel guilty if they don't "chicken soup" everyone who comes into their orbit. The challenge is to decide what is immediate and necessary and then to stand back and allow others to share in the assumption of responsibilities.

Spirituality—The quest to find a spiritual center may be all-encompassing for entities pursuing a spirituality theme. When the full potential of this theme has been reached, these entities are far-sighted, compassionate, and magnanimous, but while still involved in the search, these entities must guard against being narrow and judgmental in their views.

Survival—For any number of reasons, real or imagined, life is a constant struggle for those who've selected a survival theme. At their best in a crisis situation, these souls take a grim view of day-to-day existence. The obvious challenge here is to lighten up.

Temperance—Very probably the entity with a temperance theme is dealing with an addiction of one kind or another. The challenge here is to avoid extremes. Perhaps the entity has conquered the actual addiction but is still dealing with a residue of feelings about it. The key to combatting the fanaticism that often characterizes those with temperance as a theme is moderation—the true meaning of temperance.

Tolerance—Entities choosing the tolerance theme must be tolerant about everything—world affairs, relatives, children, politics, and so forth. The burden is so great that they often will only choose one area to tolerate, remaining very narrow-minded to all the rest. By recognizing their theme, these entities can meet the challenge and so grow more and more magnanimous.

Victim—These entities have chosen to be sacrificial lambs. By their example—dramatically displayed by the media—we are made aware of injustice. Jack Kennedy is an example of one pursuing a victim theme—not merely his means of exit, but his back pain, his family name, and the pressures placed upon him by his parents. Many victims, after having played their parts, may choose to rewrite future scripts by altering their masochistic tendencies.

Victimizer—People's Temple leader Jim Jones was a prime example of the victimizer theme in action. Within the framework of one's own viewpoint within one life, it is almost impossible to see the full purpose of Jones's manifestation of this theme, yet it is obvious that many lives, as well as many life themes, interacted with his. In the tapestry of life, Jones's unique role may have been to focus public attention on cult abuses.

Warrior—Entities with a warrior theme are fearless risk-takers who assume a variety of physical challenges. Many go into some form of military service or law enforcement. With humanitarian as a secondary theme, they may be particularly effective. Though it is important to temper aggression, it still remains that without warriors we would be prey to tyrants.

Winner—Unlike those entities with infallibility as a theme, to whom everything comes easy, winners feel compelled to achieve. They strive to win with great tenacity, often gambling or entering contests. Perennial optimists, they are always certain that the next deal, the next job, even the next marriage will be the best. No sooner has one deal fallen through than they pick themselves up and go on to what they know will be a winning situation. President Eisenhower was a positive example of this theme. As a general, his unfailing optimism was inspiring; as a president, his confidence had a calming effect. The challenge for these entities—which Eisenhower appears to have met—is to take a realistic approach to winning.

Unlike some Eastern reincarnationalists, Sylvia does not believe that reincarnation endlessly evolves through all eternity. She is certain that it stops for an entity when he or she has learned everything necessary on this planet. Her own current life is her last one here, Sylvia believes, but she stresses that this does not in any way imply perfection on her part. After many lifetimes here she has learned her earth lessons and will pursue her perfection on the other side, where she will assist some other entity as a spirit guide.

CHAPTER ELEVEN

Medicine and the Medium

THE doctor is stymied. His patient does not respond to treatment. What to do?

For the internist, the response may be, "Let's run another series of tests."

For the psychiatrist, "Back to the couch."

Either course, the patient must spend more time and money before a cure is effected.

Now, at last, there is an alternative—the psychic.

Sylvia's link with the medical community was forged in an unexpected way. Just prior to undergoing minor surgery at El Camino Hospital in Mountain View, California, she looked up at her anesthetist and informed him, "Your wife's going to have an automobile accident. I see her crashing into something. I think it's a phone booth. She'll be okay, but the side of your car will be bashed in."

The doctor was obviously not impressed. "Fine, thank you very much," he replied, "now just relax . . ." The last thing that Sylvia remembered before fading out was his condescending smile.

As it turned out, the joke was on the doctor.

When Sylvia regained consciousness a few hours later, he was sitting beside her bed. "How did you know?" the astonished man asked. It seemed that as he had left the operating room, a call had come from his distraught wife. She'd just crashed into a telephone booth.

Since then Sylvia has read for nearly half the staff of El Camino Hospital.

Before long, doctors were sending patients to *her*. Jerrod Normanly, a Sunnyvale neurologist, referred patients to Sylvia. "I had a phone call from a patient I sent to you some time back," he wrote Sylvia. "She expressed gratitude over the help you gave her. She had problems with chronic tension that just wasn't responding to various medications and other approaches.

"I must say that I consider your presence in the community a definite resource because there are certain patients who will respond to the way you deal with them far better than to orthodox medical approaches to their problems.

"I have appreciated the patients you referred to me; they have been complex to the extreme and I hope that you have been able to do something with the results of my consultations."

Sylvia now participates in a two-way referral service with some twenty-five doctors. If, while reading a client, the medium senses a specific health problem, she's able to recommend an appropriate specialist. And doctors also consult Sylvia about their diagnoses and sometimes prescribe readings with her for their patients.

Again and again, Sylvia's intuitive gift has enabled her to give inspiration to those who have lost hope, enabling them to challenge the medical establishment in seeking new paths and possibilities.

Almost any working day brings a health problem of some·kind into Sylvia's reading room. Early in 1988, a middle-aged woman entered. Before she could open her mouth Sylvia stopped her. "Don't sit down. You've got to go to a urologist right away. Do you know one?"

When the woman shook her head in bewilderment, Sylvia suggested a doctor she'd worked with before and offered to call him.

Alvin Rutner of Mountain View agreed to see Sylvia's client immediately. Two hours later the doctor called back. "That woman is seriously ill. If she hadn't come in when she did, she'd be in deep trouble. How did you know? What did you see about her that told you something was wrong?"

"I can't tell you, Al," Sylvia replied. "It wasn't anything about how she *looked*." She struggled for an explanation, but gave it up. "I just knew—how do I know anything?"

Sylvia's files are jammed with testimonials. Karen Guy of San Rafael, California, is an example. She wrote, "My skin has improved since you stressed no dairy products and L-Phenylalanine. Blood tests showed that I did have too much iron in my blood as you stated. And it wasn't until I got home that I realized that you were right in what you said—I *do* have 'flukey' periods."

A mother wrote, "My daughter wanted a baby more than anything else in the world, but couldn't seem to get pregnant. She went to doctor after doctor but no one was able to determine the cause. Finally, she came to you for a reading. You said that her problem was an ovarian cyst and suggested she go to a Dr. Nola. Sure enough, this doctor discovered ovarian cysts and has begun to treat them."

Pat Silva of Sunnyvale has written yet another testimonial. "Sylvia was very accurate regarding my need for niacin and ferrous sulfate," she wrote. "My headaches are almost gone. Also, my memory level is way up since I started taking the iron you suggested."

And Jean Turner of Fremont, California, wrote, "You were right about my allergy to dairy products. Since I stopped using them I look and feel much better."

A more dramatic case was that of Sue Lange, who had attended a seminar given by Sylvia in Santa Rosa, California. During a question-and-answer session, Lange asked about her health. Sylvia surprised her by advising that she have her thyroid checked. Lange's swollen body and inability to concentrate had heretofore been attributed to Sjögren's Syndrome, a rare blood disease. As a result of Sylvia's suggestion, Lange learned that her thyroid was indeed very low, but could easily be treated, alleviating a number of problems previously thought to be "incurable."

As the years passed, Dal Brown has developed healing powers which he makes available as a love offering to all who have need of them. He always insists that those who seek his help use it as a supplement to medical treatment. On one occasion, Sylvia and Dal were able to work together on a healing.

The case was that of Maria Tsunoda of Sunnyvale, who came to them on August 29, 1981. Mrs. Tsunoda had been diagnosed as having cancer in the bone marrow of both hands. She was in constant pain and was unable to perform the most routine chores. While Dal perfomed a healing, Sylvia worked with the patient on hypnotic programming to alleviate pain and stress.

On September 7, 1981, Mrs. Tsunoda reported that she'd had no pain whatsoever since her interview and was feeling wonderful. Ten days later she called to tell Sylvia that her doctor had advised her that she "no longer had any cancer present anywhere" in her body.

On another occasion, when Sylvia was lecturing on therapeutic hypnosis in Marin County, California, a former subject, Sue D., rose from the audience and described how a lump under her arm had disappeared as Sylvia worked with her hypnotically on a drinking problem.

Rarely is Sylvia able to help members of her own family, but a dramatic exception occurred on November 29, 1980. Her nephew, Crisjon, was taken to Kaiser Hospital in Santa Clara, where his condition was diagnosed as osteomyelitis. The treatment was to be three weeks of continual intravenous injections in the hospital followed by three weeks bed rest at home.

But Sylvia began to have very strong feelings that something was amiss. "It's all wrong," she told Sharon. "Crisjon doesn't have osteomyelitis. He has aseptic necrosis—the treatment shouldn't be nearly so extreme. Get him out of there. You'll feel better about it if you take him to a doctor named Marvin Small, but I promise you the disease will run its course in ten days. He'll only be out of school for two weeks."

Sharon and her husband, Richard, succeeded in getting their son discharged from Kaiser Hospital over many strenuous objections from the doctors there. Crisjon was taken to Small, whose X-rays confirmed Sylvia's psychic "diagnosis." The boy did have aseptic necrosis. Within ten days he was completely recovered and four days later was back in school.

The healing may take many unanticipated turns. One morning, Sylvia studied the woman who'd just sat down before her and "saw" that her client was mortally ill. "You know, don't you, that you have cancer?" she said, a statement rather than a question.

"Yes"—the woman nodded—"but what I don't know is how much time I've got. The doctor has some radical treatment that he wants me to try. The side effects are very unpleasant. If there's no hope, I'd rather be left in peace to enjoy my last days."

"If you take the treatment, you'll have six months to live," Sylvia said without hesitation. "If you don't, you'll have three."

The client sighed. A difficult choice was suddenly easy. She would decline the treatment.

Her death was an easy one, her last months uncomplicated by difficult, expensive treatments that would have brought nothing but pain. She and Sylvia talked often about her transition. When it came, the woman was ready to walk into the light.

Winifred Woods received comfort of a very different nature.

In 1978, Woods, who had muscular dystrophy, had been told that she could die at any time. She had had a series of colds and had recently suffered from flu, which had developed into a severe case of pneumonia. Having barely recovered, she was told that the next malady would in all likelihood be fatal.

One morning, Woods lay in her bed watching a favorite television program, *People Are Talking*. The face she saw smiling out at her from the screen was that of Sylvia Brown. For a time, her numerous problems were forgotten as she watched Sylvia "reading" members of the audience.

A man had risen and was challenging Sylvia. "You told my wife some things—they were sort of true, but I still don't believe this stuff . . . My father and I haven't spoken in years—"

"And that isn't going to change," Sylvia interrupted him. "He's one of those people who always has to be right so you're automatically wrong. Besides, there's another person involved, a male family member. It's a three-way ego conflict."

The man had looked surprised. "Yeah, that's true," he admitted.

"Sure it's true, so now I'm true about your wife and I'm true about you, so shut up and sit down," Sylvia said, grinning at him impishly and he laughed back at her.

A little of Winifred's depression lifted as she found herself chuckling along with them. Before she realized it, she was watching eagerly and when the program ended, she jotted down the address of the Nirvana Foundation as it flashed before her on the television screen. The doctor had said that she could die at any time, but wouldn't it be nice to know how much time she really had? Winifred thought of the fence mending she wanted to do, the affairs that could be put in order. Impulsively, she reached for a pen and paper lying beside her bed.

A few days later the answer came. To her surprise, the letter was anything but the death sentence she'd envisioned.

"Your death is far, far in the future," Sylvia had written. "Don't even think about it. You have more to do in this life."

Woods looked up from the letter and caught her reflection in the mirror. The woman she saw was glassy-eyed from medication, her body badly bloated. She felt like a helpless blimp, but how could she not feel that way? From the very beginning her doctor had said that her disease would grow progressively worse until she was completely helpless. Now she'd reached the point where her right hand was having difficulty managing a fork and her left was too weak to hold half a sandwich. And her recent siege of respiratory ailments had left her physically and emotionally exhausted.

Winifred Woods studied her reflection, searching for the woman she'd once been. If I'm not going to die, that means I've got to live—really live, she reasoned. I've got to begin taking control of my own life.

Her eyes wandered down to the throw that lay across her knees. The binding had come loose and she'd been waiting for someone to mend it for her. Next thing Woods knew she'd wheeled herself over to the cupboard where her old sewing basket was kept, found a needle and thread and secured the binding herself. The small incident proved a turning point.

Woods blamed the medication she was taking for her sluggishness. It's my life, she decided, to heck with the doctor! She cut the dosage and within days was feeling clearheaded and optimistic. A few weeks later, she'd gone from a size twenty-two to a size fourteen and was looking and feeling better than she had in years. The fingers that had had difficulty with utensils were busily crocheting an afghan. She didn't feel "sick" at all!

Wonderful as all that was, it wasn't quite enough. Sylvia had said that Winifred Woods had something to accomplish. The woman wondered what it could be. Though still confined much of the time to a wheelchair, she was getting about, doing some of her own housework, taking charge of her life in a way that no one had thought possible. Woods began to meditate. It wasn't long before an old longing resurfaced. Years before she'd written a newspaper column and planned one day to write mystery novels, but instead marriage and a family had claimed her attention. Now there was plenty of time, but could she write?

The meditations continued until an idea came to her and she set to work. The mystery novel was half completed when Sylvia came to the area to speak. Woods, with the help of her daughter, was able to attend. During a question-and-answer period following the lecture, the aspiring author was one of those called upon. Woods was so excited that she forgot to tell about the health prediction that had come through. Instead she asked, "Will my project be a success?"

"Yes, your *book* will be a success," Sylvia replied.

As of this writing, Winifred's book has been completed and is being readied for publication.

Sylvia has been able to bring insight into mental and emotional problems as well as physical ones. Thomas Peters, a Campbell, California, psychiatrist, has worked with Sylvia since 1975. "We have consulted with each other freely about families, adolescents, and children in need psychologically and emotionally," he says today. "Her liaison with the medical profession has been outstanding. In the psychiatric and psychological area, Sylvia's intuition has been particularly useful to me in terms of diagnosis and insight into family dynamics."

A few years back, Sylvia became aware that her eyes were rapidly deteriorating. "What's the matter with me?" she asked Francine.

The reply was simple. "There are too many things you don't want to see," Francine told her. After many years of psychic diagnosis, Sylvia is in enthusiastic agreement with the theory that many illnesses are caused by emotional factors. Once these are recognized, steps may be taken to correct the condition and heal or at least alleviate the medical problem. What is it that I don't want to see? she asked herself when the eye problems appeared to accelerate.

The answer seemed quite clear—problems confronting Sylvia daily in the reading room.

Perhaps on some level she was tired of leading others around and wanted someone or something to lead *her* for a change. But since this is Sylvia's chosen work, all she can do is recognize the strain and make a conscious effort to distance her inner self from it. The condition now has stabilized.

Sylvia is certain, too, that the weight problems she has suffered for many years are the result of "carrying" others in her effort to protect them. Smoking, an addiction she has conquered, represents to her a subconscious desire to hold evil at bay—a modern-day replacement for the bonfires of old.

This provocative theory extends to many areas of possibility. Sylvia perceives upper-respiratory ailments as an immediate response to trauma. You "cry" and sniff with a cold, but if you don't succeed in getting the problem "off your chest" something more serious may develop—such as pneumonia or possibly even breast cancer.

Not enough "sugar" or love may result in low blood sugar or hypoglycemia. Too much sugar—an unrealistic

Pollyanna approach to life—could result in the opposite, diabetes.

Back problems? Who or what are you carrying around?

Arthritis? Could it be that your energy is bulging at the joints?

Is your heart "broken"? Look out, a heart attack could result.

Mouth problems? Too much mouthing off. Does your blood "boil" at times? Better calm down, high blood pressure may result. And so it goes.

Once when Sylvia was attending the National Congress of Regression Therapists, she and James Fadiman, president of the Association of Transpersonal Psychologists, were discussing their health problems. "I've had a bladder infection on and off for four years," Sylvia had complained. "What do you think causes it?"

"You're smart enough to figure that one out," the psychologist reminded her. "What do *you* think?"

"I don't know. I've tried everything, one specialist after another, but I just keep getting one case of cystitis after another."

"Okay, if you can't get the answer now, drop it. But tell me, how's your family?"

"Terrible!" Sylvia fairly exploded. "That mother of mine, she really pisses me off!"

"Well, there you are!"

The two friends looked at one another and laughed, but the moment that Sylvia said the words, she knew that her bladder problems were over. Once her mind had made the connection, the healing took place.

Sylvia has since been able to use that insight again and again to help her clients. "Who's the pain in your neck? Your husband? Your children? Your parents?" she asks often with startling results.

The list goes on and on. Dizzy spells? What's keeping you off balance?

Back problems? Who's on your back? Bleeding ulcer? Who can't you stomach? The possibilities for healing are endless.

Sylvia is certain that the anxiety that causes these reactions results from the soul's need to expand. The instinctive reaction of the conscious mind to the spirit's challenge is, No, you don't. It responds, she believes, out of fear of the unknown.

The solution comes, Sylvia believes, when we consciously allow the soul to give birth to a new self. When the devil is named—when the ailment is acknowledged and the connection recognized—the healing can begin. It all comes down, she is certain, to assuming personal power. Just how readily we give that away is illustrated by the story of a client who, when given a penicillin shot by her doctor, immediately felt better until informed that the shot wouldn't take effect for at least twenty-four hours.

According to Francine, chronic pain "grooves in," continuing to send its signal long after the inflammation has run its course. Her suggested method of dealing with a traumatized nervous system is to respond to it by saying, "I have received the signal, I now produce my own anesthetic." It's like talking to God and saying, "That's enough. The groove is too deep and I don't want to put up with it any more."

Sylvia's spirit guide also urges that we prevent pain before it starts by being more self-centered, more caring for ourselves. "In doing this," Francine says, "try for one week to do everything that *you* wish to do—just for you. For one week try it. I guarantee that by the end of the week you will not only be doing for yourself, but you will be doing for more other people than you ever have before. The reward of self takes very little effort, but it brings a wealth of love that begins to emanate in all directions."

In response to Sylvia's suggestion that this might be "selfish," Francine responded that there is no such thing as selfishness—there is only fear that causes a person to become introverted and closed off to others.

In order to enable all of us to not only make the connection necessary to reach the cause of our illnesses, but to effect their healing, Francine has transmitted the Laboratory Technique.

"The Lab," she says, "is a special place where you can go to receive healing, counseling, or help with any type of problem. As you know, on my side thoughts are things. When you mentally construct your own Lab, we on our side can see it and then go there with you in order to help with problem solving. *But you must create that reality for us.*"

THE LABORATORY TECHNIQUE

In your mind's eye, build a rectangular room of a size that feels comfortable and right to you. Leave the far wall open. From the windows you will see a beautiful view of water—the sea or perhaps a lake—which will add power to the healing. Also visualize three walls of a soothing green color. In the center of the room, place a table, large enough for you to lie on. Give the table some "character," with carving or other type of ornamentation.

The more detail you give to your room, the stronger its existence will be for you. So decorate it with furniture, paintings, and other objects of art that you like. Now place a stained-glass window in the open wall. This can be of any design, but the colors must be bright—blue, purple, gold, and green in big blocks or bands.

After you've finished mentally constructing the Lab, walk through it. The best time to do this is at night as you are going to sleep. But please complete the Lab *before* falling asleep; otherwise there won't be any Lab to use. When you enter the Lab, stand in front of the glass window and allow each of the colors to penetrate your mind and body.

The blue brings tranquility to the soul and spirit, increasing awareness. The gold is for heightened dignity and intellect, the green for healing, and the purple for increased spirituality.

Allow the shining colors to enfold you in warmth and happiness. Try to actually see each as it enters you and cleanses your soul. Now ask for the white light of the Holy Spirit to surround you and make you well. Feel yourself starting to become whole now, with a new feeling of stability, power, and control in your life.

Go to the table and lie down, still wrapped in the glow of God's love. Ask the master teachers and doctors on our side to work on a specific area of your body. Though you can always ask to be relieved of mental and emotional pressures, work only on one physical problem each session. Surrender yourself totally to these spiritual helpers, for they come to you directly from God. Once you've created the room, placed yourself on the table, and identified your problem, it's all right to fall asleep. Actually, you may have a hard time staying awake because the Lab itself has an anesthetic quality.

Use the Laboratory for any problem in your life. You may also bring a loved one into your room for a healing. First you create the room mentally. Then place your person in the white light of the Holy Spirit, then put your "patient" on the table. Ask the master teachers to help with the problem.

There is no limit to what you can do with this phenomenon. The only block you may encounter could arise because the individual you desire to help doesn't want that help. If you find that this is the case, then release yourself from the trauma by recognizing the free choice of another.

CHAPTER TWELVE

The Psychic Detective

S AN Mateo County coroner's investigator Bob Jesson was angry. The last thing he wanted to do was consult a psychic. "The boss said to call you," he admitted, the irritation apparent in his voice. "We've got two bodies and no I.D. on either."

"Yes, yes, I see them," Sylvia soothed him. "One woman's short and dumpy, the other's tall, a brunette with a heart tattooed above her left breast."

"Where *are* you?" Jesson demanded, looking into the phone, down at the floor, then up at the ceiling. "Is this some kind of joke? Where are you hiding?"

"Just calm down. Listen to me a minute. I'm trying to help you," Sylvia reassured him.

"But I didn't even tell you they were women," Jesson retorted angrily.

His confusion faded as he heard Sylvia say, "Just listen while I sort them out for you. The young one's a brunette. Her name is Vivian—yeah, Vivian. I can't seem to get the last name—check the missing person's files in Petaluma. The short woman—her name's Clover—is from Monterey."

Within twenty-four hours, Jesson had verification from both Marin and Monterey counties. Two missing-person cases had been solved.

Gary Boozer, a sergeant with the Santa Clara County Sheriff's Department, was another skeptic. He'd reluctantly sought Sylvia's help with a homicide case. "Forget about that for a minute," Sylvia had advised. "I've got something much closer to home, officer—closer to *you*. It's drugs."

"I'm in homicide, not narcotics," he'd reminded her.

Sylvia shrugged. "What can I tell you—you're going to make a big drug arrest. There's a brown two-story building with a kind of rundown trellislike railing. It's an awful-looking place with writing sprayed on the walls. The street has some kind of bird name. It's off Evelyn Street. There's no grass or anything in front—just dirt—it's a mess." Sylvia paused, warning, "Watch out, you could get killed there."

Two weeks later, Boozer was unexpectedly transferred over to the narcotics division. Only a few days later, while driving down a side street, he slowed to read an address. It was Lark Street, he noted. Ahead was the Evelyn corner, to the right a brown two-story building with a railing. Remembering what Sylvia had said, Boozer decided it was the wrong place for him to be alone. He drove off, intending to survey the house later with his partner.

Within an hour, Boozer got a call. There had been a shooting in the house; one man had been killed. He returned immediately to investigate with reinforcements and discovered a cache of drugs on the premises. The arrests that he made that day put a narcotics ring out of business.

As a result of many such successes, Sylvia had been asked to speak to a number of law enforcement groups resulting in many working relationships with police officers. Gary Robinson of the Los Altos, California Police Department is one. Robinson was so impressed with Sylvia's presentation at a meeting of the homicide investigators in Sunnyvale that he called her regarding the notorious "ski mask rapist," a man who'd been terrorizing the entire San Francisco Bay Area for three years.

Twenty-six women, ranging in age from sixteen to eighty-three, had been brutalized, though the police believed that there were many more victims who'd been too terrified to file a complaint. Police teams throughout the area were frustrated in their many attempts at apprehension because the criminal never left fingerprints or used a car that could be traced. He said little to his victims and only two of them had seen his face, for he invariably wore a characteristic blue ski mask. Adding to the mounting terror was the rapist's uncanny knack for knowing when his victims would be alone. The assaults most frequently occurred in schoolyards, but women had also been violated in their homes, in vacant office buildings, and, in the case of the oldest victim, in the confessional booth of a church. Invariably, the rapist threatened his victims at gunpoint, bound them, and, after sexually assaulting them in a variety of ways, demanded cash, jewelry, or automatic teller cards.

"What can you tell me about him?" Robinson asked Sylvia.

"I can see him!" she exclaimed, overcome, as always, with excitement at her vision. "He's husky, dark haired, white, but somewhat Negroid looking. I can't quite get the name, but I know the last name begins with *S*." She paused momentarily, then continued more slowly, "I realize that it sounds kind of funny to say a rapist is gentlemanly, but in a way he is."

Robinson looked up from his notebook, eyeing her intently. "What do you mean?"

"I don't know, really. It's like I said—crazy as it sounds, it's like he's almost polite about it."

"It does sound crazy," Robinson agreed, "but several of the victims have told us that even though the guy threatened to kill them and showed every evidence of meaning it, he was apologetic. 'I've killed before and I can kill again, but I'm sorry' sort of thing. There's never been anything in the newspapers about this trait, but it's a theme that keeps coming up again and again in each of the victims' descriptions." Robinson was eager now, leaning forward. "Anything else? Think about it . . . some little detail. Never mind if it sounds crazy."

Sylvia nodded. "Yes, there is something else. He works for the city."

"That's pretty broad. I do myself. What do you mean?"

"I don't know exactly what he does. It's like he draws lines on the street—or else he works *under* the street. Yeah, under the street, but there are lines connected with it someplace. He does something with lines. I don't get it."

"Neither do I," Robinson said as shook his head. "Anything else?"

"It's going to happen next in Redwood City," she told him. "You better start doubling up in Redwood City, because that's where you're going to catch him. He's thinking about Redwood City. He wants to rape someone there, but instead you'll get him."

On November 30, 1987, a cold Monday night, police caught George Anthony Sanchez—the man with the initial *S* that Sylvia had "seen." The twenty-six-year-old San Jose city sewer repairman was breaking into a Redwood City home where a woman was living alone. A search of Sanchez's home and vehicle revealed possessions belonging to victims of the ski mask rapist as well as a second ski mask similar to the one he was wearing.

One hundred and one felony charges were filed against the man, who is currently serving a lifetime sentence.

Though Sylvia feels an obligation to use her psychic gifts to assist the police whenever possible and has frequently volunteered her services to them without charge, she is well aware of the risks involved. For this reason she tries whenever possible to maintain a low profile.

Francine, who frequently assumes a protective mantle, has suggested that Sylvia begin each day with a prayer:

> Father/Mother God, I ask that the White Light of the Holy Spirit surround and protect me this day and every day. I ask that it cleanse and purify my soul. I release to the light now any negativity as so much dark smoke to be absorbed by the White Light, causing no one harm. Let nothing but love and positive energy pass into or out of this protective bubble.

Sylvia had difficulty truly feeling this prayer until she remembered Glenda the Good from *The Wizard of Oz*, who always appeared within a clear bubble. With that image in mind, it was easy for her to envision a similar shield around herself and so evoke the White Light. Now Sylvia includes her family within the protective bubble as well.

Though much of Sylvia's time is spent assisting law enforcement officers in the apprehension of criminals—she calls it being a psychic detective—she much prefers locating missing persons. A frequent function here is "simply" a matter of providing much-needed solace to distraught loved ones.

One day, Mary Ellen Stewart of San Jose contacted the medium. Frantically, she described the details of her daughter Marion's disappearance. "Is she all right? Where is she? Will she ever come back?"

"Yes," Sylvia reassured her. "I see her—I see her clearly. She left of her own volition and she'll come back when she's ready. She'll come back in March."

On March 29, 1983, Mary Ellen Stewart called again, her voice choked with emotion. "You were right," she informed Sylvia. "Marion came home this morning."

Sometimes Sylvia is able to provide tangible information that facilitates the search. In 1987, Maria Elena Ulery called about her missing daughter. "She's fifteen, she has reddish blonde hair, braces on her teeth—"

"Sure, sure, I see her," Sylvia interrupted. "She's with two friends—a blonde girl, I think her name's Kathy, and Kathy's boyfriend. The boy has dark hair and blue eyes. Kathy's parents don't want her to see him. Do you know who I'm talking about—that small blonde girl, Kathy?"

"Yes! Yes, I do," Ulery gasped.

"Talk to her parents, they know something that will help you," Sylvia advised.

A short time later the medium received a note from the much-relieved mother: "Thanks very much for your help at the very moment that I needed it so much. What you told me was right. You helped me through the most terrifying moments of my life. My daughter is back and I hope I can find a way to guide and to help her."

Sometimes the police use information received by Sylvia to recover a missing child. One such episode involved Sarah Jane Dalitz, who'd been missing for two years despite repeated efforts of law enforcement officers to locate her. The grieving mother despaired of ever seeing her child again until Sylvia told her: "Sarah Jane was kidnapped by a man who seems very fond of her."

"Can you see him?" the detective asked. He'd been reluctant to accompany Dalitz to Sylvia's office but now was suddenly eager. "Describe him—what does he look like?"

"Yes . . . he's short and stocky with a lot of sandy hair," Sylvia replied.

"Why, that's my ex-husband!" Dalitz responded, fairly shrieking.

"You never thought he might be the one?" the detective asked.

"No, I really didn't think he cared that much . . . It's a relief to know that Sarah Jane's safe, but I want her back. Imagine him putting me through all this!"

"Do you know where he is?"

"No," Dalitz said, shaking her head, "I've no idea. It's been so long since I heard anything from him."

A map began to appear before Sylvia's mind's eye. "She's in the Northwest." A state began to stand out, and finally, a city. "It's Seattle," she announced, "Seattle, Washington."

Dalitz looked blank. "So far as I know there's absolutely no connection to my husband. He's never worked there, he's got no family there, no friends."

"Why not give it a try?" The detective shrugged. "We've tried everything else. Let's give it a shot."

Two days later the two flew to Seattle. Within a week Sylvia received a call. "You were absolutely right," the happy mother reported. "She was in Seattle living with her father, but now she's home with me."

Not all Sylvia's psychic searches have such happy endings. It is always difficult for a medium to report tragedy to a hopeful loved one, but at least there is the awareness that the waiting, the uncertainty is at last at an end. One such case received nationwide coverage.

In the late spring of 1982, Milton Tromanhauser went off into the wilderness to meditate. The fifty-three-year-old Martinez, California, building contractor was a deeply religious man. He had traveled extensively in India and the Middle East and could quote the Bible in depth. Tromanhauser had fasted in isolated areas many times, believing that this enhanced his meditations and furnished him with insights into the problems plaguing mankind. Each year the mystic made a pilgrimage. That summer Tromanhauser's goal was to fast for forty days and forty nights. No one knew his destination.

The pilgrimage had begun May 10, 1982. When forty days had passed, Terri Ball, a close friend of Tromanhauser's, became alarmed. She first called the East Bay Regional Parks ranger who referred her to the Contra Costa County Sheriff's Department who sent her to the East Bay Regional Parks security division who added to her growing frustration by suggesting that she again talk to the Sheriff's Department. This time the Sheriff's Department sent her to the Martinez Police Department. By now she was desperate.

"Perhaps someone would pay attention to me if I could tell them exactly where to look," she appealed to Sylvia. "Part of the problem is that he never told me where he was going. Last year he climbed Mount Tamalpais in Marin County. Do you suppose—"

"No," Sylvia stopped her. "Not Marin, he went to the east—Contra Costa County. The place where he is—it's called devil something—devil—Devil Mountain?"

"You mean Mount Diablo?"

"Yes, that's it," Sylvia exclaimed, then hesitated. "I'm sorry to have to tell you this, but he's dead. He's been gone for some time. You'll find his body in the water."

When the Contra Costa Sheriff's Department scoffed at the idea of a psychic sighting and refused to follow up on this lead, Terri Ball enlisted the aid of two ranchers, who went into the wilderness area on horseback. Within three hours they'd found Tromanhauser's body floating in a small spring on the slopes of Mount Diablo.

Terri Ball's agonizing vigil had come to an end.

Though Sylvia does charge for psychic readings and hypnotic regressions, she refuses to take any payment for her police work or for her efforts to locate missing persons, believing that it is her obligation as a psychic to help those in need. "How can I possibly make money from the grief of others?" she asks.

In another volunteer project, Francine provided the information for one of the medium's most unique assignments. William Yabroff, a psychologist and associate

professor at University of Santa Clara, approached Sylvia
with this challenge. One of his graduate students was working on a project involving suicide victims.

All the student knew about the ten people involved was
what she had read in the papers, and the details were very
sketchy. A man might have shot himself, but where? In
the head, in the chest? A woman might have died of an
overdose, but what was the drug used? The purpose of
the study was to find out more. What were the motives
behind the act and exactly how did the death occur?

So Yabroff brought his student to Sylvia's office at the
Nirvana Foundation. Sylvia's husband, Dal, placed her in
a deep trance. Very slowly, gradually, they began to feel
another presence and, of course, it was Francine.

When the spirit indicated her readiness, only the ten
names were submitted to her one by one. Sylvia, Yabroff,
and the student knew only that the names belonged to
suicide victims, but they had no other information. This
lack of knowledge on their part was intentional and important. It eliminated the possibility of mind reading.

As each name was provided, Francine unhesitatingly
described in detail the circumstances of the case. Not only
was she able to say exactly when and where the deaths
occurred, but she also pinpointed the motivation and its
evolution and the exact method used, including, in one
instance, a complex drug compound.

Then shortly before the trance ended, Francine spoke
directly to the young graduate student. "George is here
with me on the other side," the spirit informed her. "He's
very anxious that you know that his death was an accident.
His gun discharged by mistake. There was absolutely nothing that you could have done to help him."

The young student gasped in astonishment. There were
tears in her eyes when she and Yabroff left. Yabroff later
described their departure to Sylvia. "What was that all
about?" he'd asked as they drove back to the university.

"I suppose it's the whole reason that I became involved in the suicide study," the student told him. "I'd been a volunteer at a crisis center. One night a man named George called and told me he was going to commit suicide. He said he had a gun in his hand. I talked to him for a long time and I thought I had him talked out of it. Then suddenly there was this noise—it was horrible. I knew that he'd shot himself. I've thought so many times that it was my fault, if I'd been better—if someone else had talked to him—perhaps it wouldn't have happened, he wouldn't have done it. I've felt so guilty—"

It was a very happy young woman who was able to verify Francine's descriptions with the San Jose District Attorney's office. Francine had been entirely correct about the time, place, and motivation for each of the deaths. Nine of the ten described were correct as to every detail. In the case of the tenth, Francine had said that the man had shot himself in the head when in reality it had been the chest.

In stress situations, those involving unusual demands, Sylvia often retreats to her own "temple of quiet," a special meditation technique, an ultimate refuge. She regards it as being of particular value where missing persons are concerned.

THE TEMPLE OF QUIET

Begin by calling on your spirit guide and entreating him or her to take you to the temple. As you approach, you will see a short flight of stairs before you. Climb those stairs, then enter the eminence of the temple.

The floor at first looks like marble blocks, but as you advance toward the center of the room you will see that each block emits a beam of light that centers on you.

THE TEMPLE OF QUIET *(continued)*

Each is quite lovely. Some are pink, others mauve, blue, and green.

When you reach the center of the room, ask that your dilemma be resolved. As you phrase your request, an octagonal crystal set in the wall before you will emit a beam of light into your third eye. As this occurs, the circumstances of the problem will be re-enacted before your eyes and all available options will be revealed to you.

You can enter the temple with any kind of problem— a lost or endangered loved one, job conflicts, tests, finances, personal relationships. You can program the resolution of the problem any way you please, but first view all the options.

For example, suppose you lose a job. What is the next option? What about a better job, or possibly an opportunity to change careers? Ask that a variety of options be played out before your third eye like a movie scenario. Then select the resolution that feels best to you.

When dealing with a stressful situation you may want to say, "What is the worst thing that can happen?" You may be surprised that the "worst" is really not so terrible and even that possibility can be reprogrammed to something better.

Remember, you can always reconstruct characters and situations in a manner that will contribute to your evolvement. Make certain, though, that you consider the evolvement factor in your planning. Remember that we are all interconnected and each of us has a right to determine in accordance with our free will. Each person is his own chairman!

CHAPTER THIRTEEN

Novus Spiritus

O N April 12, 1986, Sylvia looked out over the capacity crowd at the Flint Center in Cupertino, California. It was question-and-answer time.

A small gray-haired woman called out, "Will my marriage stay together?"

"Bite the bullet. Hang in there," Sylvia advised her. "September will be the turning point. Be patient just a little longer. It will be worth it in the long run."

A younger blonde woman rose from the audience. "My husband's going into business—" she began. But Sylvia stopped her. "Are there two other people involved—a man and wife?" When the woman nodded excitedly, Sylvia was emphatic. "No, *no*—don't do it! Don't let him do it!"

A small dark-haired woman in her late twenties waved her arm eagerly. When Sylvia nodded at her she was suddenly reluctant. "Yes, yes—go ahead," Sylvia urged, "you can ask me anything."

A faint blush tinged the woman's cheeks as she faltered. "My—my boyfriend—he and I have a son. Do you think—will we ever—"

"Get married?"

The woman nodded vigorously, then broke into a broad smile as Sylvia continued. "Yes, you will and I think you'd better hurry up about it because there's a daughter on the way."

"You mean I'm pregnant now?"

"If not now, then in the next ten minutes," Sylvia said over the laughter of the audience. "*Really*, I'm only half-kidding. You better get on with the marriage soon. It's a little nicer that way, better for the kids, easier for them later on."

"What about you, Sylvia?" a man seated far in the back of the auditorium called out. "What's coming up for you?"

The medium's reply was characteristically matter-of-fact. Looking out over a sea of more than two thousand faces, she announced, "On the way over here I decided to start a new religion."

And she did.

At that moment, Sylvia embarked upon the most important chapter of her life to date. The symbiotic result of her devotion to God and her prophetic gift is Novus Spiritus, or "new spirit." The religious organization was founded to serve individuals who find no reasonable explanation for life, who seek another dimension to their faith, or who are confused or put off by traditional religion.

Novus Spiritus differs from Western theology in three major areas. First of all, it represents the return to the belief in reincarnation, which was an integral part of Christianity prior to its drastic restructuring under Pope Constantine at the Council of Nicea in the sixth century.

Secondly, Sylvia's church is unique in that it is the first religion in more than twenty-five hundred years to embrace the female, as well as the male, aspect of the deity. The Mother Goddess is alive and well in Novus Spiritus. She is coequal with the male, the emotional dimension as opposed to the pure intellect of the male principal. Combined, the two comprise the Godhead.

Finally, and perhaps most important, the new religion provides a forum for the expression of the love and joy that is God without fear, guilt, or punishment. Through her church, Sylvia hopes to give the world a means of understanding the always-benign God of life and human existence.

"For the record, God is blameless," she reminds her congregation. "She/He is not prone to the human traits of vengeance, hate, or just plain crankiness. He/She is constant, pure, a loving intellect. God does not sit around all day, then suddenly invoke damnation on a helpless person. *Never.*

"There is no room in Her/His perfect being for such nonsense. Inherent in the perfection of the deity is a steady love for His/Her creations, a never-wavering compassion, and a constant companion along the way. Whatever you experience, God too has felt it, right by your side. For within you lies a spark of the Divine. God is simple; people are complex."

It is within this complexity that evil arises. "Evil is *not*," Sylvia stresses, "a creation of God. From simple adversity, evil has developed into the concept of the devil, complete with horns and a tail—a mythological being in direct competition with God. In reality, evil is merely a logical opposite to the concept of good.

"Since every person has an innate knowledge of good, it's inevitable that each must also possess an awareness of its direct opposite. All through our lives we are constantly choosing between the two modes of expression. The parable of Satan tempting Eve—Eve means 'life' in Hebrew—to partake of knowledge closely parallels the Novus Spiritus interpretation. Only by living and facing adversity can one perfect one's soul—that is, know the difference between good and evil."

"Why a church, Sylvia? Aren't you busy enough already?" many asked in the early days of Novus Spiritus. The answer was yes, of course, she was and is. Sylvia does between eight and twelve readings a day and may receive more than a thousand letters and calls within a week. Additionally, she participates in numerous research projects, missing-person searches, and volunteer work with the police department. She also teaches ongoing classes in hypnosis, counseling, and psychic development.

The Nirvana Foundation now has more than twelve thousand members, and Sylvia is assisted by a staff of fourteen. Among them are Sylvia's sister and brother-in-law, Sharon and Richard Bortolussi, as well as Barbara Crowther, the wife of the police officer who urged Gary and Sylvia Dufresne to come out to California so many years ago. A very significant member of the team is Sylvia's younger son, Chris, who has inherited her psychic gift and has been doing readings on a full-time basis at the foundation since 1983.

Novus Spiritus grew out of a need. "I can't find what I'm looking for in any church," clients complained to Sylvia again and again. "I was raised on Sylvia Brown philosophy. It's what I believe," a young woman said one evening at a foundation meeting. Then she asked the question that set everyone to thinking: "Shouldn't it be accessible to more people?"

"It's not *my* philosophy—at least not originally," Sylvia was quick to remind her. "I'm only the channel. What I've shared with you over the years is Francine's wisdom, the knowledge of the other side." That night, Sylvia was awake a long time. Since 1974, she had received thousands of pages of information culled from hundreds of deep hypnotic trances. These transcripts, catalogued and cross-referenced by members of the Nirvana Foundation, had formed a tremendous knowledge base not available from any other source. Wasn't it her obligation to share these unique spiritual insights with anyone who might desire them?

The responsibility seemed enormous. Just being a medium was often a burden. People imagined that she was perfect. As the founder of a new religion, her followers would expect a saint.

"You are always yourself, Sylvia," Francine reminded her. "No one grows by leaning on someone else, yet everybody seems to be seeking a guru to direct them. You are very honest about your frailties to everyone who cares to listen—on the radio, on television, and from the lecture platform. How can anyone ever do an exposé of you? You've already exposed yourself!"

It was all quite true, Sylvia realized. She was forever pounding away at the fact that she, like everyone else, had needs and emotions of her own to deal with. She was *very* human. All her life she had been required to follow her blueprint from day to day, just like everyone else. The insights she received from Francine were always for the enlightenment of others, not herself.

It had finally become quite clear to Sylvia that the new religion was the realization of her long-term humanitarian dream, the enactment of her karmic theme. There was no question about it. After having absorbed so much of Francine's otherworldly perspective, it was obvious to her that traditional religions no longer addressed the needs of today's world. The insight was so startlingly clear that she wondered why she hadn't realized it earlier. Hers was a clear call to refine and promulgate the wisdom that she'd received from Francine. Perhaps a degree of her own perfection and refinement might come from dealing with the criticism she would undoubtedly encounter for following this controversial path.

The basic tenets of the new faith were revealed by Francine. First, of course, was the practical task of forming the credo itself. Soon Sylvia realized that she could do this coincidentally with the beginning of her ministry. "Our culture cannot live by rules set down two thousand years ago," she pointed out at her first service, or "celebration." Sylvia's message reflected her confidence.

"The fact is that human intellect grows and the capacity for learning grows with it. We need an *intellectual* basis for God. Novus provides that basis. Does it really matter whether you wear jewelry? Does it really matter if you practice birth control? Does it really make any difference whether you go to church every Sunday? Is dancing really an instrument of the devil? Come on, *think*! Do such restrictions matter an iota in the grand scheme of life or, for that matter, in the evolvement of your soul? Novus Spiritus thinks they don't. Two thousand years ago Our Lord said: 'Love your neighbor as yourself.' We all got the neighbor part. We don't always do it but everyone agrees we *ought* to. The self part we ignore because we equate self with selfishness. It doesn't mean that at all. Loving ourselves means nothing more than the essential awareness of the God Center within ourselves and of our inner connectedness with God and with each other.''

What makes Sylvia's church truly unique is the total absence of fear or guilt, for Sylvia—and Francine—believe guilt to be counter to both life and to a living, breathing religion. Novus Spiritus is a practical, portable philosophy, a viable belief system applicable to all the trials and the triumphs of everyday life, a religion that can accompany one anywhere in the world. Though it's reassuring to enjoy the camaraderie of church services and to respond to the inspiration of the sermons, one does not, according to the tenets of Novus Spiritus, have to go to church to find salvation. Salvation exists when that fruition is reached entirely within one's own heart.

The way of all peace is to scale the mountain of Self. Loving others makes the climb easier. We see all things darkly until love lights the lamps of the soul.

Those words form the first tenet of Novus Spiritus. Within them lies the basic philosophy of the church. Life is discovery—a long, long journey of discovery, wherein everyone must meet and love themselves, overcome individual fears, and learn the great truth about loving. It is a process of perfecting the innate, God-given beauty of the soul.

The journey for most takes numerous lifetimes to achieve. Novus Spiritus embraces reincarnation. "How could it be otherwise?" Sylvia asks. "Perfecting one's soul is the most important task that each of us ever performs. It is more than a task, it is the continuing life process. Consider how most of us learn. Isn't it almost always by trial and error? We do a new task repeatedly until we do it correctly—even the most trivial tasks require repetition. Has anyone ever tied their shoes on the first try?

"But then are we to assume that God has no patience with us? Will She/He be upset if we are not perfect after merely one life? Would His/Her anger condemn us to roast in hell because tying our shoes took a whole month to learn? We think not. Reincarnation is the most reasonable concept to explain the inequities of life in the light of an all-loving God. The alternative—a God of hate—is simply not tenable."

Every person, indeed every sentient being, can be likened to a newspaper reporter working for God, the editor. The whole reason for life is to witness for God all of Her/His knowledge—this, indeed, *is* life. Along life's journey we must learn the meaning of being good and, in so doing, perfect our souls.

The concept of perfection is very much a part of the Novus Spiritus creed, as is the knowledge that each of us is obligated to perfect our souls. No one is expected to reach the ultimate perfection of God. The idea is for all people to reach the level of perfection that they have chosen, with which they will be content through all eternity.

Francine has used the analogy of the thimble and the bucket to illustrate this point.

A thimble and a bucket both stand empty. Each must realize its full potential. The bucket begins its journey through life. As the waters of experience are added, the bucket slowly fills. The little thimble then starts its journey. In a short time the thimble has filled itself and is content. Yet the bucket has much more work to do until it too stands full. Now which one is the fullest?

The answer, Francine reminds us, is neither. Both are full to the brim, and that is sufficient. The fact that the bucket contains more is not important. The goal is to seek and find a level of perfection that exactly fits *you*. Upon reaching that level, you are full—as perfect as you can become.

Naturally, we must give full credit to the bucket. Obviously, it has learned a great deal—which is very important to the bucket. In the course of its labors, the bucket enjoyed a richer understanding of many things. More insight, more beauty, more knowledge are available to the bucket. Yet this does not mean the thimble is unfulfilled or unhappy. Indeed the thimble cannot even conceive of those things which the bucket most treasures. The thimble is completely happy with its own level of perfection and cannot be happier. It's really a matter of capacity.

As of this writing, the Church of Novus Spiritus has one thousand members. In addition to the mother church in San Jose, there is now another branch in Burlingame, California, and plans are being made for a third branch in Los Angeles. Thirty-five ministers have been graduated from Sylvia's two-year course with a new class now under way.

Much of the church's sentiment can be found in this communion prayer:

Dear Mother and Father God:
    We ask you to witness this communion, which is a symbol of finding our own God-centeredness and Christ-consciousness.

In doing this action of taking bread and wine, we are impressing on our higher consciousness that we are dedicating our lives to God's will.

The symbol of this communion for us through Novus Spiritus means we wish to be born into the new spirit of true spirituality and let go of all guilt and karmas of our past lives and start fresh and new. From this time forward, we will be on track fulfilling our themes and walking with the blessed aura of God's Light.

We do this as an activation of our will to symbolize to ourselves and the world that we walk in grace, free of all negativity.

We ask this in Your name.

                                                                    Amen

Services are warm and intimate. There are simple prayers and hymns. Sermons are practical and to the point, invariably dealing with issues of personal and national concern, such as battered wives, AIDS, or teenage pregnancy. An integral part of the service is the meditation, during which the congregation sits quietly with palms upturned while Sylvia or one of her ministers points the way toward self-healing, goal achievement, or other desired paths.

Another important part of the service is the healing that is given to all who seek it. Those desiring healings may also ask to have their names added to the prayer list. A group meets each Wednesday evening at the church to pray and send healing energy to those on the list.

Sylvia's files are jammed with letters from men, women, and children who have been helped in this way. An example is Eleanor Moore of San Jose. Moore had been diagnosed by her San Jose gynecologist as having an ulcer on her urethra. She was referred to a San Jose urologist, who informed her that an operation was necessary, and a date for the surgery was set. But in the meantime Moore, though in great pain, attended a Novus Spiritus service and requested a healing. Almost immediately she felt better. Later in the week, she called the church and asked for a remote healing from the prayer group.

A few days later she returned to her doctor for her scheduled examination. "I *knew* I was healed," she said later, "but I still went through the motions. My doctor confirmed my feelings but insisted that I be examined again by the urologist. I agreed and once again the two doctors agreed, but this time their joint decision was 'No operation.' I didn't need one; I was completely recovered."

In addition to holding weekly services and prayer meetings, Novus Spiritus ministers maintain a twenty-four-hour crisis line, offer spiritual counseling, hypnotherapy, meditation classes, and provide convalescent home visits and car-pooling services for the elderly and the handicapped. Plans are now under way for an AIDS hospice to be funded by Novus Spiritus.

Sylvia's very special partnership with Francine continues to unfold from day to day. Novus Spiritus is in every sense a living religion where the word of God is often revealed on a daily basis. As the ability to comprehend grows, new and deeper truths are manifested. For years Francine has been saying, "If you think of a question, the answer will be found."

Sylvia's challenge is to provide those answers.

Tenets of
Novus Spiritus

THE tenets form guidelines for living and embody the philosophy and research upon which Novus Spiritus is founded. Since some of the concepts may be new to many, the following will help to clarify them.

I   *The Way of All Peace*

. . . is to scale the mountain of Self. Your journey through life is largely one of self-discovery. Life is designed to test the very mettle of your soul. The largest obstacle is the self with all of its doubts, worries, and inhibitions. To truly be your *self* it is necessary to break through the limitations we have imposed upon ourselves. The best way of doing this is to focus energy outward to others. By getting out of yourself, you will find yourself.

II   *Love*

Love is a force; it is the perfect emanation of good as defined by God. No love is ever lost. If you put love into the world it is absorbed by someone or something that can use it. Love also has a way of coming back to you, although you may not always see it. Love will always hit the mark. Though people may choose to ignore love, it always leaves an impression.

   You can test this for yourself. Make a conscious effort to beam a shot of love to someone. Do they react? Does something change? Sooner or later it will. Try sending love to strangers, watching them closely. You can always love the spark of the Divine within people, even when you don't particularly like them.

III *Purity*

God is pure and constant in Her/His love, while people are erratic and subject to petty behavior. Never ascribe to God such pettiness, for it is not in Her/His nature.

Negativity abounds in the world. Did God create it? No. People alone are responsible for it. Through free-will choice, some will invert good to make negativity. Choosing between light or darkness is one aspect of your path to perfection.

IV *Creator*

You are an actual part of God, carrying within your soul a spark of the Divine. This spark has marvelous abilities, largely untapped, to perform miracles. The most pressing need in this world is to make it your heaven. Call upon the strength within, allowing this innate goodness and beauty to mold the world around you. Let your God-center view life as a heaven, control negativity, do not allow it to control you.

V *Power*

Call upon the spark of the Divine and consider it a veritable force at your disposal. Most of us have experienced turning the power outward, perhaps when your "heart went out" to someone in need or when loving someone— often a pet. You can actually feel an emanation leaving you. It is the very heart of God moving. Cultivate this power, turn it outward, help others with it.

VI *Faith*

Faith is a tool. When the world is darkest and you are struggling to survive, faith can get you over the worst. The best application of faith is to trust in your own strength and in God, your constant companion. Have enough faith to turn to God for help. And always know this: You are never asked to endure more than your soul can take. Every prayer is answered.

VII *Life*
Life is a sojourn, usually alone, during which you perfect your soul for God. The result of all your suffering is to be content with yourself, knowing the true meaning of goodness. By your own volition you will not rest until that day. In the meantime, simply survive each day and you will ultimately succeed. Learn from each step, better yourself on the next step, and you will recover your lost perfection.

VIII *Judgment*
The soul cannot be judged by anyone but God. Let no person claim to have dominion over your spirit. We can judge the acts performed by people, and be subjected to social law, but none of us is qualified to judge the soul.

IX *Light*
Let the innate beauty of your soul provide a beacon for others in this world of darkness. Show others how to live, and be an example for them. Choose joy, show a zest for life, love others, and make your own heaven. Light your lamp for them all to see. You will find it can change your path and hasten your perfection.

X *Growth*
Reach outward and grasp God, then find the God within yourself and join together. Forge the bond between your Creator and yourself. Live and actualize this bond. In so doing, your spirit will soar, fear will vanish, and life will become a joyous path leading home. Let God's love enter your spirit and magnify His/Her presence.

XI   *Communion*

Purge any notion of demons, sin, devils, or bogeymen. The only demons in this world are self-doubt, insecurity, and the fear of being unworthy of God. God is perfect love and we are his children; therefore everyone is worthy of His/Her love and our own. Certainly we have imperfections, but those will be dealt with in time. God does not withhold His/Her love until you attain perfection— She/He would be very lonely if that were the case.

The concept of "sin" has a very tragic history. Novus does not believe in sin (or karma) as touted by most religions. The fear of sin has caused centuries of grief and problems for people. It is time to correct the definition.

We feel that "sin" can only be committed against *ourselves*. It occurs when an individual willfully and maliciously endeavors to harm another. Certainly the victim is harmed—and that is unfortunate—but the soul of the victim is not injured. Only the soul of the perpetrator carries a scar and only God and that individual can determine the proper restitution. There is no damnation and everlasting hellfire. The soul itself will seek to rectify any injustice, with a loving God for guidance.

Unfortunately, some churches claim that any deliberate turning away from God, however slight, is a "sin" and will jeopardize the soul. That is nonsense for it implies that God is so vindictive as to disallow normal human emotion such as anger, distress, and pain. The fundamental nature of God is love, which in itself implies forgiveness. Can a moment of emotional passion be a "sin" to the One who created us? Never, for we believe in an all-loving God.

XII   *Divine*

God created us with a body, the mechanism to live in this world. The glorious part is that within the body lies a part of Her/Him—that aspect of us called the soul. This spark of the Divine is worthy of all the respect given to God.

XIII *Perfection*

Does God send damnation and pain to you? Never. Do you send such things to yourself? Yes, to provide obstacles that aid in the perfecting of your soul. Those having many trials in life are perfecting faster by their own choice. Others, of course, may elect to take it more slowly but the end result remains the same. We will all arrive at a point of self-contentment and remain forever with God in our true home which is the other side.

XIV *Karma*

Karma is a simple balance of experiences. If you were poor in one life, you may want to try being rich in another. If you have experienced being ugly, you may choose another time to be beautiful. A former cripple may return as an athlete. Every person will select the required balance of experience. There is no such thing as "bad karma" being inflicted upon anyone. The only judgment comes from yourself and God—and only you two can balance any inequities.

XV *Reincarnation*

The primary goal of living is to perfect one's soul. It is the single most important job that we do. Does it make any sense to give it just one try—pass or fail—for all eternity? No, not if you accept a loving God. Indeed, most "mysteries" of religion will disappear when reincarnation is added to the mix. And that is precisely why the early Church Fathers, at the Council of Nicaea in A.D. 325, burned overt references to reincarnation, fearing it would erode their power.

Novus Spiritus believes that God is all-loving and provides a means to correct our errors, for the path to Him/Her is harsh and varied and we will stumble often along the way. An all-loving God will take our weakness into account and assist in making us whole.

God does not condemn babies and aborigines to hell because they were not "saved" before dying. Every person will have many opportunities to live in this world. Each life brings us closer to perfection until eventually no further lives will be needed. The true concept of being saved is to reach that level of perfection ordained by both you and God.

XVI   *Meaning of Life*

Do you need a meaning in life? Most have some vague notion of needing to serve. But how? Some folks sublimate this urge by working to achieve business success, yet may find their achievement empty. Others seek fulfillment in political power or wealth. All of these are secondary to the reason for living. Indeed, a simple formula for success is to live for God, love others, and be a beacon of hope to the world. Therein lies achievement.

XVII   *War*

An act of war is wrong, for overt killing defiles the temple of God. However, when attacked, it is compulsory to defend that temple. Never be afraid to strike back when your life, your way of life, or your loves ones are threatened.

XVIII   *Death*

Death is the reward of living. You have spent your time in the physical world with its negativity, heaviness, and loneliness. Now comes the good part, when you can return home to the true existence and be welcomed back into the direct and ever-present grace of God.

Never fear dying. Even if you feel damnation awaits you, *it does not*. The grace of God will counsel and heal you. Then, when proper, you will face another life to balance your soul.

Avoid prolonged use of artificial life-support systems. Allow the spirit to leave when the body is spent. Death is never an accident.

HIDDEN POWERS OF THE MIND